Stitchery

EMBROIDERY
APPLIQUE
CREWEL

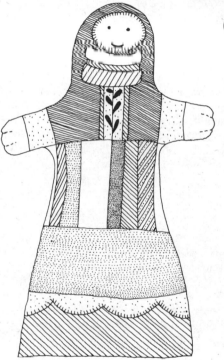

By the Editors of Sunset Books

Lane Publishing Co. • Menlo Park, California

Foreword

For centuries stitchery in its many forms has been employed as an embellishment for fabrics of all kinds. Essentially a *hand* craft, embroidery adds a uniquely personal touch that may be even more satisfying than the completed project it is decorating. Whether sophisticated and slick or gently rustic, embroidery provides its own rich counterpoint of color and texture.

This book is meant to be an introduction and guide to the basic techniques of stitchery.

We would like to thank all of the people who have generously shared so many hints and suggestions by answering our request in *Sunset* Magazine for embroidery and applique ideas, as well as those who offered their fine stitcheries for use in our book. Special thanks to the following individuals for their extra efforts and encouragements: Kay Aronson, Ruth Baldwin, Lyndane Browning, Roberta Fanning, Nancy Freeman, Doris Hoover, Melissa Hougham, Alberta Humphreys, Cecile Huntzinger, Araby Judd, Marilyn Judson, Tina Kauffman, Nancy Lawton, Sylvia Matthews, Mrs. Nelson T. Nowell, The Peninsula Stitchery Guild, Joan Schulze, Audrey Thorup, Margaret Vaile, and Kelly Wallace.

Research and Text: Lynne R. Morrall
Supervising Editor: Alyson Smith Gonsalves

Design: Michael A. Rogondino, JoAnn Masaoka

Illustrations: Nancy Lawton

Front Cover: Sunshine sampler (page 44), chain of flowers work shirt (page 50), and Russian princess doll (page 65). Photograph by Glenn Christiansen. Cover design by Roger Flanagan.

Back cover: Photographs by Glenn Christiansen.

Executive Editor, Sunset Books: David E. Clark

Third Printing March 1975

Contents

The many faces of stitchery

The term "stitchery" has come to mean almost any handiwork done with needle and thread—from the simplest flower embroidered on a knee patch to an applique and yarn landscape that has the sparkle of a freshly painted watercolor. It can also describe a stuffed and machine-stitched Daliesque canvas flower pot or a crewel tapestry completed after seven years of loving labor.

All of these projects, in fact, were done with great enthusiasm by stitchers of different ages and backgrounds. Yet all radiate the special feeling of freedom and joy that working with thread and fabric can give. Each tells a little about its creator's personality, both in the form of the finished article, and in the differences in small detail.

Three approaches to one design

Like handwriting, stitching is individual, both in the kinds of stitches people make and in their choices of color. Give a group of people the same design to work with and they will come up with very different finished products. The example on page 5 illustrates this point. Three people were given a piece of linen stamped with the same design and were asked to work it with their choice of thread, color, and stitches. The finished products have blossomed into three very individual expressions. One has a three-dimensional look, another is done entirely with shiny floss, and the third is a strictly traditional piece of crewel work.

"But," you say, "those three people are obviously experienced, professional embroiderers!" Yes, but each of them started with *one* stitch, and so can you.

How to begin

Start with a scrap of fabric, needle, and any thread or yarn that will fit the needle's eye; more sophisticated tools can come later. Stick the needle into the fabric and start sewing—in and out—and your work will soon begin to grow. Try a backstitch (a concise stitch, clear and clean)

Jeans hip pocket *displays embroidered tendrils, flowers, and butterfly; French knots punctuate flat felled seams. Design: Tina Kauffman.*

Silver thread *sleets wetly across a tulle and organdy sky above Death Valley in this applique and stitchery "painting." Transparency of the fabrics used creates subtle color changes. Design: Margaret Vaile.*

Delightful variety in materials and interpretation characterize these three examples taken from a series of ten floral basket renditions. Yet each began as one of ten identical designs stamped on linen. Design: Elsa Williams Company. Courtesy Southern California Chapter of The Embroiderer's Guild of America Incorporated.

in a straight, then a curved line, writing your name in script. Use a pencil to sketch in the curves if it makes you feel more secure.

When you grow tired of doing a particular stitch, stop and pick up a new stitch or go back to one you like. Many projects can be made with only one stitch (see the crewel belt buckle on page 56). If you want a bold patch of color, pin a piece of felt on your material and applique it with fancy and plain stitches, playing with different colors, shapes, weights, and textures of yarn or thread. Make up stitches or try combinations or distortions of stitches to form texture: for example hills and valleys of satin stitch, punctuated with French knots. March along with fishbone, write with backstitch, and enjoy the freedom of

Seven years in the making, thread-encrusted crewel tapestry depicting Adam and Eve in the Garden of Eden is a stitchery extravaganza. Design: Constance Hunt.

chain stitching. Work these stitches in different weights and colors of yarn as an experiment in color and texture.

Try doodling with the needle and thread. One stitchery devotee wears the overshirt she is appliqueing, taking it off to work on while waiting for appointments. Pulling out fabric scraps, needle, and thread from her purse, she begins adding new patches. When she has to stop, she carefully clips and secures the ends of the thread, puts her materials away, dons her shirt, and goes on her way. The kind of shirt she is creating may appear too large a project for the novice. But remember, it's growing slowly. When queried about her shirt, the lady replied that she had never planned to cover the whole thing with patches but found stitching such fun she just couldn't stop.

Hopefully this creative "bug" will spread to you, once you've tried some preliminary stitches.

If you're a perfectionist at heart, you might enjoy the discipline of creating a sampler (see page 44). Once it's completed, you can make it into something useful, such as the wall hanging shown on page 49. But if this approach doesn't suit you, try playing randomly with thread or yarn on a scrap of fabric. Do whatever feels most comfortable. Stitchery—unlike crochet or knitting—allows you to put your work down and then pick it up again hours or days later without worrying about its unravelling or about losing your place in a long list of directions. Another advantage to this kind of needlework is that, with the exception of sampler work, where stitches are lined up for inspection, mistakes in stitchery aren't as obvious as those in knitting and crocheting.

If you *are* intrigued by now, you'll be interested in one of the projects illustrated on pages 44 to 79. Or if you need help on the preliminary steps to stitchery or techniques, move on first to the information given from page 6 to page 41 before tackling your chosen project. Change the color scheme if you like, enlarge or reduce the design, or combine ideas, but try to choose for your first project one you think would be most fun to do. And now that you're on your way, the best advice is this: don't talk about it, *do* it.

Getting started in stitchery

Of the several approaches to learning stitchery, the most common is the sampler, a piece of fabric containing rows of different stitches—a kind of catalog of all the stitches you know. Two types of samplers are shown in the projects section of the book (see pages 44 and 54), one of which particularly appeals to children (see "The Underground Sampler," below). Included also are other hints for children's work and for left-handed stitchers.

Your Own Sampler—the Traditional Way

Use the traditional sampler to master basic stitches, referring to it later as a sort of "stitch dictionary" when you begin to design your own embroideries. You could start with a basket-weave sampler, such as the one shown on page 49, making small groups of the same stitch and watching how they relate to one another. Or you could follow the collar project shown on page 53—a sampler of free-form shapes.

Both are traditional samplers that provide you the same time-honored opportunity to learn stitchery, but they are quite different in character and appeal. The basket-weave sampler could be made into many objects: a purse, pillow, or decorative wall hanging. The collar can be worn with a simple sweater or embroidered as a decorative yoke on a blouse or dress.

The "underground" sampler

Let's face it—some people are meant to live by rules within lines and spaces and circles, and some aren't. If you aren't, here is an alternative to a disciplined sampler. Play around. Practice one or many stitches until you're pleased with their looks; then put them right on your project. Throw this practice cloth away when you finish or keep it as a free-form sampler (so you'll have a record of the stitches you know—for reference).

This method of teaching stitches is especially pleasing to children who often lack the patience to embroider rows and rows of the same stitch.

Basic sampler supplies

To begin, choose a soft cloth with a fairly loose but regular, even weave. Natural or synthetic linen, hopsacking, and synthetic burlap are all good choices because each has a weave that separates easily and allows a blunt needle to pass through.

For yarn, pick something easy to work with that will show off the stitches well, such as pearl cotton number five; a corresponding needle would be size 5 crewel.

An 8-inch wooden embroidery hoop is a comfortable size to use when working on most projects. For more information on this and other choices, see "Supplies" on pages 9 through 11.

Choosing colors

Since this sampler will be your first attempt at stitchery, choose your favorite colors when selecting yarns and fabrics. Keep in mind that the fabric color should show off the stitches to their best advantage, but, above all, pick colors you'll enjoy working with. Many people rejected stitchery as small children because they were forced to

Samplers have been used as teaching tools for many years. This example dating from 1792 was worked at the age of 10 by Betsy Wheaton of Leicester, Massachusetts.

complete a tedious sampler before going on to something "fun." Let the sampler become a labor of love, not a piece of drudgery.

Children's Stitchery

Since some children will even shy away from the doodling sampler technique, preferring to start right in on a project of their own, a good stitch to teach them with is the chain stitch. Quick and easily mastered, it is more interesting than a plain running stitch.

Burlap makes an inexpensive "canvas" for children to begin with, and bright bits of yarn leftovers provide a surprisingly complete palette. This method was used in the example below.

Some children prefer to work from a drawing; others like to draw a quick sketch in chalk or pencil on the fabric before beginning. To teach a child to transfer a drawing, follow the directions given on pages 12 to 13.

Stitchery equipment for children

Just as a child likes to choose his own color combinations for his first drawing, so may he wish to choose his own yarn and fabric for his first stitchery. *Your* job will be to make the right kind of equipment available to him so his first attempts will be successful and encouraging. Here are some suggestions:

Needles. Small children find large needles, like large pencils, easier to use. The needle should be slightly thicker than the yarn so it will open the fabric for the yarn to pass through without strain.

Needle substitute. Wrap the yarn end with cellophane tape or dip it in white glue to make the end stiff. This makes a nice substitute for a needle when used with loosely woven fabric, hardware cloth, or screening.

Yarn. Cotton yarns snarl less than wools. Of the cottons, pearl cottons are twisted and produce a smooth, even surface, whereas stranded cotton floss, which can be separated, tends to pull unevenly and make loops on the surface. Since long strands of yarn and thread tend to tangle and fray, begin with 28 inches or less to avoid any uncomfortable arm-stretching.

Fabric. Any open-weave fabric is suitable (see the photo on page 10 for examples). Also suitable are hardware cloth and window screening, which can be used like needlepoint canvas—covered with stitches and bent into three-dimensional shapes. Before you begin working with them, bind the edges with masking tape.

Hoops. Six and eight-inch wooden hoops are sizes that children can handle. Wooden hoops are adjustable for different weights of fabric and will not pop apart as spring-type metal hoops tend to do.

If you don't wish to use a hoop, you may want to stiffen the fabric with spray starch or sizing.

Sewing box. Use a shoe box or basket to hold yarn, needles, scissors, two small pieces of soap or wax (see "Techniques", below), dressmaker's chalk, scraps of fabric, beads, and metallic thread. As time passes, your child will probably add to this collection.

Techniques

Stitchery techniques for children are not very different from those followed by adults, but here are a few helpful tips:

Threading the needle. Before threading the needle, moisten an end of the thread in your mouth, lay it between the two pieces of soap or wax, and then pull the thread out. This will stiffen and flatten it, helping to ease it through the eye.

Knotting the thread. Traditionally, embroidery and crewel threads are not knotted but instead woven back into the fabric. Some children find this technique tedious and frustrating. If so, teach them to knot the end of the yarn by wrapping it two or three times around the index finger and then pulling it off by twisting it between the thumb and index finger.

Left-handed Stitching

Left-handed embroiderers will have little trouble executing stitches because most stitches are worked the same way by both right and left-handed people.

But some improvisation may be necessary. Line and border stitches sometimes will need to be reversed. To do this, simply hold a mirror up to the drawing illustrating the stitch and work from the mirror image. Another approach is to follow the steps by turning the book upside down. When in doubt, first practice the stitches step-by-step on a scrap of material.

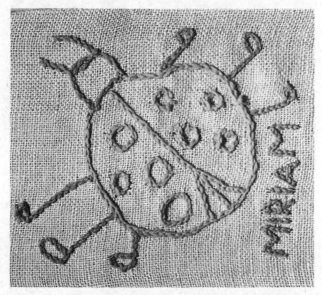

"Drawing" with chain stitch on burlap is easy and fun for a child. At age 5, Miriam created this friendly ladybug. See *"Children's Stitchery"* above. Design: Miriam Kirkman.

Stitchery supplies

The basic stitchery tools used in all the projects in this book are inexpensive and easy to obtain. You can find them in variety stores, department stores, and fabric shops. Imported or domestic yarns and other materials are stocked by yarn, needlecraft, and import shops. For listings of these shops, consult handweaving and craft magazines and the yellow pages of your phone book.

Just seeing the vast array of beautiful colors and textures displayed in craft shops is inspiring to both beginning and advanced stitchers. A well-stocked yarn basket can be very stimulating and, like well-stocked kitchen cupboards, can eliminate frantic, last minute shopping trips.

Begin with a Needle and Thread

This section will give you specific information on needle and yarn sizes and how they interrelate. But remember, this is just a guide. Most experienced stitchers don't think much about the kind or size of needle they're using.

In choosing a needle and thread, the most basic rule to follow is to pick a needle with a large enough eye to hold your thread. It should also make a hole large enough to allow the thread to slip through the cloth without dragging against it. Some stitches are easier to execute with a blunt needle, primarily those that are woven, whipped, or laced on the surface of the fabric (see pages 16 to 25 for more information).

Needles

The smaller the needle's number, the larger the needle. This applies to all four needle groups: sharp, crewel, chenille, and tapestry. For a comparison of needle sizes, consult the chart on this page (9-A).

Sharp. These needles are of medium length, with a small eye for cotton or polyester-blend sewing thread or for a single strand of 6-strand floss.

Crewel (or embroidery). In sizes 6 to 8, these needles are medium in length and sharp, with a long eye for 6-strand floss and pearl cotton #8. Size 6 has a larger eye for tapestry wool and for pearl cotton #5.

Chenille. Short and sharp, these needles have a large eye for thick threads and tapestry wool.

Tapestry. Available in many lengths, these needles have a blunt point for stitches worked on the surface and can be used with any thread or yarn.

Yarn and thread

When choosing yarns and threads, first consider how they will be used. If they are to decorate clothing, they should be washable. On the other hand, if they're meant to be decorative wall hangings, they can be cotton, wool, synthetic, or even metallic. Cotton floss, pearl cotton, and crewel wools were used for most projects in this book, but any substitution can be made as long as it suits your needs and the finished project's function. Here are a few of the many kinds of yarns and thread available:

Cottons. The best choice for the beginner, cotton yarns are inexpensive, washable, and available in a wide range of colors and weights.

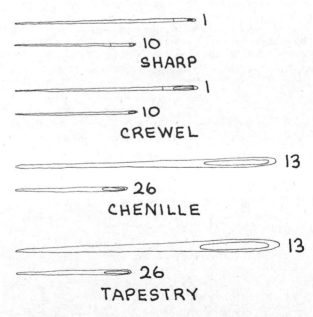

9-A. Stitchery needles *can be divided into four categories: sharps, crewel, chenille, and tapestry. Shown here are the smallest and the largest needle sizes in each category.*

Suitable fabrics for use as backgrounds for stitchery would include the following (*from left to right*): felt, cotton-and-flax hopsacking, natural linen, cotton muslin, 100% rayon linen-type weave, cotton and flax blend drapery fabric, 100% jute burlap, and rayon-cotton drapery fabric. Each provides a crisp backup for stitches.

Cotton floss is probably the most accessible of all embroidery threads. Sold in variety stores, fabric shops, and department stores, it is made of six strands of fine thread and can be used as is or divided into one, two, or three strand groupings, depending on the effect desired. Satin stitch (shown on page 22) is generally done with a single strand when a very precise, smooth effect is desired. When used with all six strands, cotton floss tends to pull unevenly and make loops on the surface but will give a weighty, almost plushy finished effect. Made by several companies, domestic and foreign, flosses vary considerably in quality and price. The more expensive variety comes in a wider range of colors and has a glossier surface but is more difficult to find (needlework shops do carry it). But it's foolish to skimp on supplies if you value the time spent on a project and the enjoyment of actually working with fine materials.

Pearl cotton, both imported and domestic, also comes in a wide range of colors and is sold mainly in needlework shops. Twisted (not dividable) and very shiny, it is sold in skeins or balls. The common sizes are 3, 5, and 8 (the lower the number, the heavier the thread). The sampler on page 49 was made with pearl cotton #8.

Crochet cotton can be substituted for pearl cotton. Less expensive and lacking the shiny surface of pearl cotton, it has, nevertheless, a crisp texture and launders well.

Wools. Although wool yarns require special handling when cleaned, they provide subtle colors and textures that can't be duplicated by cotton or man-made fibers.

Crewel wool comes in small packages of yarn wound on cards. The wool must be used in short lengths to keep it from being frayed by the eye of the needle.

Tapestry yarn, sold in skeins, is heavier than crewel wool and comes in a variety of rich colors.

Knitting worsted (including synthetics) and rug yarn, although not twisted as tightly as tapestry yarn, can be substituted for the tapestries.

Other yarns and threads. Don't overlook novelty threads when planning a stitchery project. But remember that some types require special handling when being cleaned. Check labels for washing instructions.

Linen thread, sold in skeins of soft colors, is sometimes hard to find but will give a tidy, finished effect.

Silk sewing thread and *buttonhole twist,* shiny and expensive, are sold on spools in fabric shops. Use beeswax to stiffen and strengthen the thread and make it more manageable (see "Techniques," pages 14 and 15).

Silk floss, sold in skeins and available in needle-craft shops, is glossy and expensive.

Rayon, made in Mexico and sold in skeins, is hard to find. Its bright, rich colors tend to unravel and tangle, but it can give a showy, splashy accent.

Metallic thread comes in spools and skeins and is available in many weights and textures (even wound around elastic). Sold in fabric shops and notions departments, it's very useful for special effects (see the stars embroidered on the quilt on page 70).

Fabrics

Any kind of fabric can be used in stitchery. Some fabrics are particularly useful for such specific projects as samplers, but any good-quality, firmly-woven material that has been preshrunk will work. Suitable fabrics are recommended for all of the projects on pages 44 to 79—except for those made with ready-to-wear clothing. Here is a listing of typical fabric choices for stitchery (see photo above).

Cottons and blends. Denim, mattress ticking, good quality muslin, homespun, and hopsacking provide good backgrounds for stitchery. Before you begin work, make sure your fabric is preshrunk.

Linen, natural and blends. The traditional choice for crewelwork ("crewel" means wool yarn worked on linen), natural linen has a unique texture that cannot be duplicated, although it does wrinkle and may need professional blocking. Linen threads can be counted for precise stitching; for example, cross stitch "legs" can be kept exactly 3 or 4 threads apart.

Burlap, natural (100 per cent jute) and synthetic. Natural burlap fades and can be scratchy and uncomfortable to work with, but it's an inexpensive material children enjoy. Although synthetic burlap is hard to find, it has a softer texture and doesn't fade.

Wool. None of the projects in this book call for wool, but it can be used for some of the clothing designs.

Hoops and Frames

A hoop or frame is necessary to minimize puckering and to keep fabrics from twisting off grain. Available in several sizes, hoops and frames range in price from about a dollar for a simple wooden hoop to $20 for a floor frame.

Embroidery hoops. Round or oval, embroidery hoops are made of wood or metal. Because metal hoops rust and are too slippery to hold fabric taut, wooden hoops held with adjustable screws are a better choice. They are available in many sizes, but a 6- or 8-inch wooden hoop is suitable for most work.

Standing floor frame and "fanny" frame. These frames enable the embroiderer to push the needle in from above with one hand and pull it through to the back with the other. Though relatively expensive and hard to find, these frames will increase your skill and speed, freeing both of your hands to work.

Artist's stretcher frame. Available at art supply stores, the stretcher bar frames used for oil painting canvas come in all sizes. Before embroidering, stretch your fabric around the frame, tacking or stapling it to the back. When your project is completed, it can be hung on the wall without any additional blocking or framing. You could use the stretcher frame for the sampler shown on the cover and on page 49, leaving a larger border of blank fabric around the edge of the sampler since you won't be able to work past the inside edge of the frame.

Sewing Basket and Supplies

Following is a list of the equipment you'll need in addition to your needles and thread:

1) A basket or box to hold small supplies.
2) Embroidery scissors with sharp points.
3) A thimble—only if you normally use one in sewing.
4) A dressmaker's carbon and tracing wheel or transfer pencil (see "Design and Transfer," page 12 to 13).
5) Beeswax or two small pieces of soap for stiffening thread (see "Techniques," pages 14 to 15).
6) Dressmaker's chalk for making guidelines for certain stitches.
7) Pins for positioning appliques.
8) Graph paper for enlarging designs.
9) Plastic bags for holding thread leftovers and for bonding applique pieces (see "Hand and Machine Applique," pages 30 to 33).
10) A small ruler or tape measure for accurate stitching and for transferring patterns.
11) A rubber balloon. Wrapped around a stubborn needle, a balloon can help ease it out of heavy or thick fabric.
12) A notebook or large envelope to hold design ideas, sketches, photographs, or magazine articles on stitchery.

Stitchery yarns come in a wide variety (*clockwise from lower left*): *wool rug yarn, light weight crochet cotton, heavy weight crochet cotton, tapestry yarn, acrylic worsted yarn, tapestry yarn by the strand, Persian tapestry yarn, cotton embroidery floss, balls of pearl cotton #5, machine embroidery thread, metallic thread, Mexican rayon floss, pearl cotton #5 in skeins.*

Pattern design and transfer

Translating design ideas into embroidery stitches and enlarging and transferring designs to fabric may appear the most difficult steps in stitchery to the beginner. But they needn't be. This section gives transferring techniques for all of the designs shown in this book, in addition to tips on finding and using designs of your own.

Choosing and enlarging your design

The box below at right suggests stitches for particular effects, such as leaves, borders, and flowers. Practice these stitches either on a sampler or practice cloth. Soon your eye will be trained to see things around you as potential embroideries: a printed tablecloth, wallpaper, an antique china pattern.

In choosing an embroidery design, consult library books on peasant embroideries and costumes of various periods. Early Renaissance paintings can offer lots of inspiration if you inspect the fine details of clothing and robes as a source of ideas for embroidered borders and braids. Once you've found a design, follow these suggestions for enlarging or reducing it:

Photostat. One of the simplest methods (but also the most expensive) for enlarging or reducing a picture or design, a photostat will provide a photographic reproduction of your design sized to your specifications. Shops specializing in this kind of work are listed in the yellow pages of the telephone book under "photo-copying" or "blueprint services." The cost will be about $4.50 for an 8 by 10 black and white print.

Opaque projector. Available at some public libraries and schools, this kind of projector can be used to magnify and project your design onto a screen. You can then trace this enlarged design onto a piece of paper.

Slide photography. With this method, you can photograph your design and have it developed as a slide. It can then be projected onto a piece of paper marked with the desired dimensions taped to a wall. Adjust the projector until the pattern is the right size; then trace.

Graph paper grid. To enlarge a design on graph paper, follow these steps: **1)** Trace the design onto graph paper or paper marked with a grid pattern of 1/4-inch or larger squares, depending on the size of your original design. **2)** Draw a rectangle around the tracing. **3)** Then draw a diagonal line through the rectangle. Place this drawing over a larger piece of graph paper, extending two adjacent sides of the rectangle and the diagonal line to the final size you want on the large piece of paper, drawing in the rest of the large rectangle. **4)** Next, count the total number of squares in the small rectangle and divide the larger rectangle into the same number of squares to form a grid (or use graph paper with larger squares than those on the first sheet of graph paper). Make tiny marks on each square where the lines of the design cross it; then

Using embroidery stitches effectively

Pages 16 through 25 list 32 popular embroidery stitches. Here are some suggestions on where to use these stitches in your work:

Borders or applique edging: backstitch, page 16; blanket, page 16; buttonhole, page 17; chain, page 18; chain of grain, page 17; split stitch, page 24; stem stitch, page 24; zigzag braid, page 25; Pekinese stitch, page 22.

Filling in large areas: brick stitch, page 16; bullion knots, page 17; double chain, page 18; chevron darning, page 18; couching, page 19; feather stitch, page 19; French knots, page 20; French knots on stalks, page 20; herringbone stitch, page 20; close herringbone, page 20; cross bars over laid work, page 21; long and short stitch, page 21; satin stitch, page 22; wave stitch, page 24; weaving stitch, page 25.

Flowers: bullion knots, page 17; fishbone stitch, page 19; French knots on stalks, page 20; lazy daisy stitch, page 21; satin stitch, page 22.

Flower stems: chain stitch, page 18; split stitch, page 24; stem stitch, page 24.

Leaves: feather stitch, page 19; fishbone stitch, page 19; French knots, page 20; long and short stitch, page 21; seeding, page 22.

Herbs, vegetables, and fruits: brick stitch, page 16; chain stitch, page 18; close herringbone, page 20; fishbone stitch, page 19; French knots, page 20; long and short stitch, page 21; spider's web, page 23; split stitch, page 24.

join these marks to reconstruct your design, lightly sketching in the outline.

To reduce a design, reverse step 3, placing a smaller sheet of graph paper on top of the drawing. Mark the outer dimensions of the reduced design on the smaller sheet and then go on to step 4, counting the number of squares in the larger rectangle and dividing the smaller rectangle into the same number of squares. Complete the procedure as directed.

Transfer methods

Among the many methods used to place designs onto fabrics, the simplest are to sketch freehand on your fabric or to embroider the design directly onto the fabric; then fill it in without using any sketch at all.

These methods are the more dependable and precise ones:

Dressmaker's carbon. Sold in fabric shops and notions departments, dressmaker's carbon comes in dark blue or purple for light fabrics and white or yellow for dark fabrics. With the design on top, place the carbon *face down* between the fabric and the design. With a sharp pencil, ball point pen, or a tracing wheel (sometimes sold in a kit with dressmaker's carbon), trace the design onto the fabric. Do not use ordinary carbon paper for this procedure—it will smudge.

Transfer pencil. Available in needlework shops and some stationery stores, the transfer pencil is used to retrace the design on the *back* side of the paper on which the design has been drawn, creating a mirror image of the finished design.

Make sure the pencil point is sharp. Place a sheet of paper under your hand to avoid smudging while tracing the design. Turn the design *face up* on the material, with the transfer pencilled side *against* the cloth. Then press (don't rub back and forth) the cloth with a warm iron. A positive image will be transferred, but the image will be permanent, so work carefully.

Net or nylon crinoline. You can trace your design onto net or crinoline (available in fabric shops) with a permanent felt tip marker. Pin the net in position on the cloth and trace the design again with the indelible marker. The ink will pass through the holes of the net to the cloth.

To make a precise transfer using any of the above techniques, follow these steps: **1)** Fold the fabric you plan to decorate in half and then in half again, finding its center (the creases will serve as guide-lines). **2)** Stretch the fabric taut on a smooth surface, holding it in place with pushpins or masking tape. **3)** Fold the paper or net with the design in half, then in half again. **4)** Center the design creases over the fabric creases, slipping the carbon paper between the two if you are using the carbon method. **5)** Hold the design down with weights (books or rocks) while transferring it. Be careful not to shift the design.

Cross stitch or geometric pattern. Mono canvas or cross stitch canvas, available in needlework shops, can be used as a precise guide for the placement of cross stitch or geometric patterns. Using the illustration at right (13-A) as a guide, trace your designs onto canvas; then baste

the canvas onto your fabric **(1)**. Embroider the design through both the canvas and the fabric, using the canvas threads as a guide for keeping your stitches equal in size **(2)**. When finished embroidering, unravel the threads of the canvas and pull them out **(3)** leaving the cross stitch or geometric pattern on the fabric. If your fabric is washable, soak the embroidery first in cold water to loosen the canvas threads and soften the sizing; this will make removal easier.

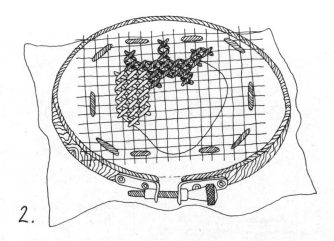

1.

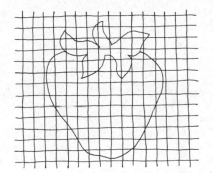

2.

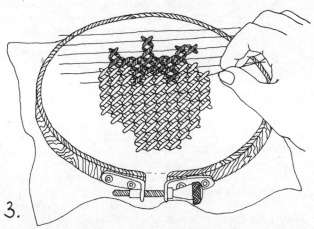

3.

13-A. Using needlepoint canvas *for placement of cross stitches: top, draw design on canvas; center, with fabric in hoop, tack canvas to fabric and then work cross stitch over canvas; bottom, pull out canvas thread by thread.*

Embroidery and crewel techniques

A picture is worth a thousand words, especially when embroidery techniques are being explained. Illustrations make learning them a quick and simple task, so follow each step given in the drawings and photos that follow. They will help you to master basic embroidery techniques. Instructions and illustrations for 32 embroidery stitches are given on the following 10 pages.

Here are a few tips to keep in mind before you begin:

1) Always preshrink the fabric or garments you plan to embroider. If you are in doubt as to whether the flosses and threads you're using are preshrunk, preshrink them, too. To preshrink materials, dunk them in a bowl of hot water for 30 minutes, drying them as you would when the embroidery's completed. Use a washing machine lingerie bag to hold small pieces of fabric and floss intact in the dryer.

2) If you plan to sew the clothing you will embroider, embroidering will be easier if you do it before sewing the pattern pieces together. First trace and cut out the pattern; then transfer the embroidery design. Using this method, you will have a swatch of fabric large enough to fit comfortably in an embroidery hoop. In planning and transferring your design, allow room for darts and other shaping in the garment.

3) If you are working with a design with lots of colors, use several needles, threading each with a different color to save time—and your patience.

4) On some stitches a blunt needle is suggested for *some* of the steps. Instead of changing needles for these steps, try pushing the needle *eye-first* through the material.

5) To achieve maximum speed and accuracy, use both hands. Stab the needle into the fabric with one hand, pulling it through with the other. If you're using the floor frame or "fanny" frame (see page 11), keep the same hand on top of the hoop and the other below it at all times.

6) Although traditional crewelwork and embroidery is done with no knots on the back of the material, most stitchers today tie a knot at the beginning and end of each length of thread. If you wish to work without making knots, work a short row of backstitches in the center of the area to be filled, hiding them later with filling stitches.

7) Wind usable scraps of yarn or thread around your index finger to make neat coils that won't tangle. Then store scraps in plastic bags in your yarn basket.

8) Yarn and thread have a right and a wrong direction, almost a "nap." Run the thread through your thumb and forefinger in one direction and then in the other. Moving in one direction, you'll feel as though you're going with the grain. Thread your needle so the thread will go through the fabric this way to make stitching easier.

9) To make thread smooth and strong and to help ease it through the needle's eye, draw the thread through two small pieces of hand soap or a piece of beeswax.

Dividing floss

You may prefer to work some stitches with a single or double strand of floss rather than with the standard six strands. To divide floss without snarling (the thread, not your facial expression), cut a length of undivided floss about 28 inches long, dividing the first inch or so into the

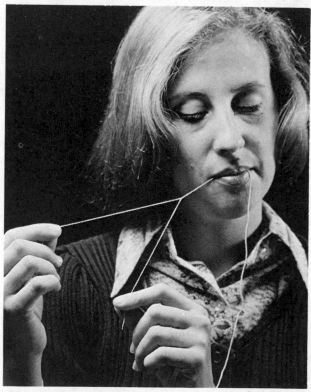

Moistening helps to separate strands of cotton floss without snarls or tangles. Pull them through your mouth to moisten; then separate free ends with your hands.

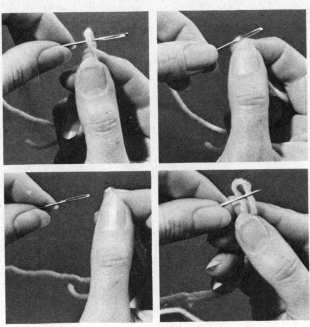

Threading the needle: top left, loop yarn over needle; top right, pull loop tightly against needle; bottom left, remove needle; bottom right, force needle eye down on yarn and pull through.

number of strands you need and whatever strands are left. Put the floss in your mouth and pull it through, moistening it with your tongue as it comes out and separates (see photo on facing page).

Threading the needle

Threading the needle, like knotting thread, can be done by following both a traditional and a more relaxed approach. The relaxed approach is to lick the end of the thread and push it through the eye. This usually works with smooth cotton threads, but with wool yarn it will leave traces of fuzz in your mouth for what may seem like hours. For wool, try this traditional method of threading the needle: loop the yarn over the needle as shown above, grasping the yarn between the thumb and forefinger and pulling it tightly against the needle. Remove the needle, forcing its eye onto the yarn that is held tightly between the finger and thumb; pull the yarn through.

Putting fabric in the hoop

Whichever hoop or frame you choose (see "Supplies," pages 9 to 11), be sure it is clean and has no rough edges (use an emery board to sand it). Always keep the fabric "square" (don't pull it on the bias) and follow these steps as shown in the illustration at right (15-A). **1)** Before assembling the hoop, adjust the screw so the outer hoop fits snugly over the inner ring; **2)** place the fabric between the two rings, centering your design; **3)** press the outside ring over the inside ring, pulling the fabric taut on grain—*not* on the bias; to release the fabric, press your thumbs down firmly into the fabric on the frame, at the same time lifting off the outer ring.

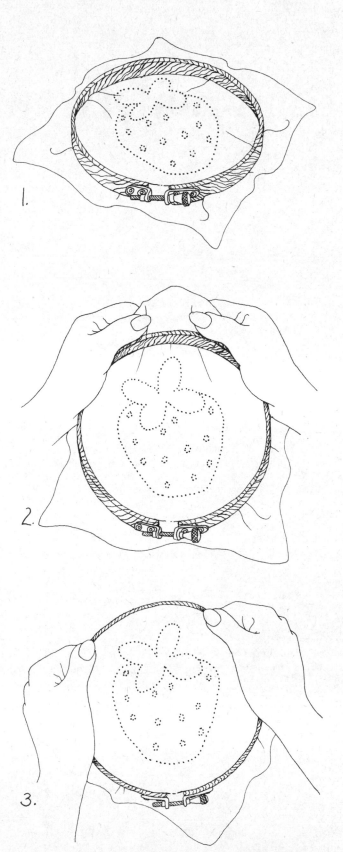

15-A. Fabric is put in hoops by *1)* placing fabric between upper and lower hoops, *2)* pushing the upper ring down with the heels of both hands, and *3)* adjusting the ring by pulling the fabric taut, being careful not to pull it off grain.

Embroidery stitches

Backstitch. Come up at A; go in at B; come up again at C. Repeat, going back into same hole at A as the last stitch. Keep stitches uniform in size.

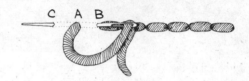

Blanket stitch. **(1)** Come up at A; go in at B, leaving a small loop. Come up again at C directly below B and in line with A while holding thread under needle (as shown) with thumb. Pull thread through. **(2)** Repeat. Also see spiral stitch, page 24.

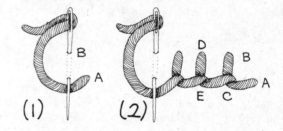

Brick stitch. **(1)** Come up at A; go in at B. Repeat in a row, leaving a space between each stitch the width of one strand of yarn. **(2)** Fill in the spaces left between the stitches in row 1. Come up at C; go in at D (these stitches should be twice as long as the stitches in row 1). **(3)** Come up into the lower holes formed by row 1, making these stitches as long as the stitches in row 2. Repeat steps 2 & 3 until enough rows have been made, ending with a row of half-size stitches the same size as those in row 1.

 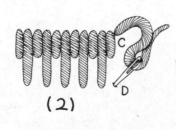 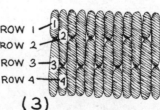

Bullion knots. Double thread works well for this stitch. **(1)** Come up at A; go in at B, leaving a loose loop of thread. **(2)** Come up again at A, bringing needle only half-way through fabric. **(3)** Holding needle from below, twist thread around needle as shown (length of coil should equal distance between A and B). **(4)** Draw needle through thread coil as shown (loosen coil a bit if necessary) while holding coil tightly with other hand. **(5)** Place needle point against end of coil and pull on thread to make coil lie flat against fabric. Stroke it with the needle to even out any bumps. **(6)** Put needle in at B at end of coil and pull through firmly.

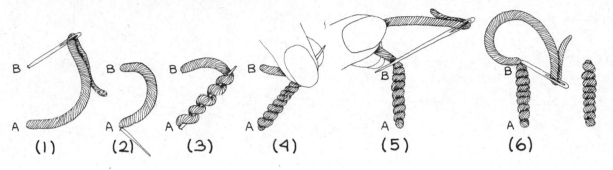

Buttonhole stitch. This stitch is worked in the same way as Blanket stitch but with stitches closer together. **(1)** Come up at A; go in at B, leaving a small loop. Come up again at C directly below and close to A. Draw thread through. **(2)** Repeat.

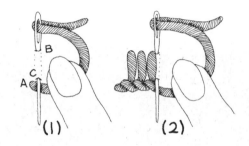

Chain of grain. **(1)** Come out at A. Holding thread to the right, go in at B; come out at C. Pull thread through. **(2)** Holding thread up and to the left, pass needle under stitch just made from right to left without picking up any material. Pull thread through firmly. **(3)** Holding thread up and to the left, pass needle under the same stitch from right to left just below the first coil. Pull through firmly. The two small coils should rest neatly one below the other. Keep tension even. **(4)** Continue with the thread held down and to the right; then go in at D and out at B (DB should be the same length as BC). Pull thread through. **(5)** With thread held up and to the left, pass the needle under the new stitch DB from right to left as before. Pull through firmly. **(6)** For the second coil, pass needle under two threads: the lower part of the last stitch and the top of the first stitch. Pull thread through firmly. You have now completed two sets of coils. Continue repeating steps 4 through 6.

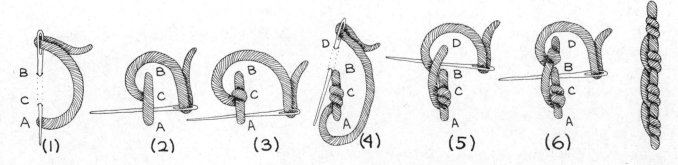

Chain stitch. Bring needle up at A. Form a loop and hold thread down with thumb. Go in again next to A; come up at B. Draw needle over loop. Do not pull thread tight. Repeat, forming a chain.

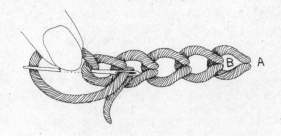

Double chain stitch. (1) Come up at A, forming a loop and holding thread down. Go in at B; come up again at C, halfway between and below A and B. Draw needle loosely over loop. (2) Go in again at A. Form a loop to the left. Come up at D. Draw needle through. (3) Go in at C within the original loop forming a third loop. Come up at E. Draw needle through. (4) Continue, looping thread alternately left and right.

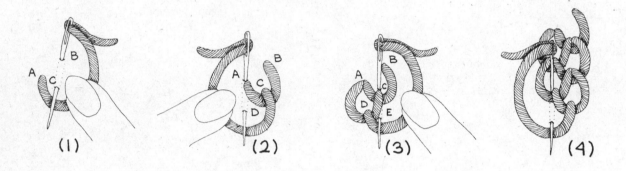

Chevron darning. (1) Draw a horizontal guide line from lower right corner to upper left corner of shape to be filled. Fill in shape by drawing parallel lines ¼ inch apart. Come up at A; go in at B, keeping needle vertical. (2) Come up at C; go in at D. (3) Continue to opposite corner, keeping needle vertical for each stitch, lengthening and then shortening stitches as necessary to fill with vertical stitches a ¼-inch wide diagonal area. Come up at E; go in at F. Continue down row, keeping stitches horizontal and altering the length of the stitches as needed. (4) Continue filling in diagonal strips, alternating between rows of horizontal and vertical stitches.

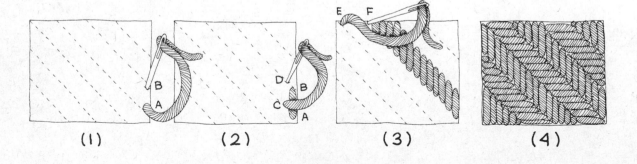

Couching. **(1)** With thumb, hold down one or more threads. With another thread, come up at A, go in at B. **(2)** Come up at C and in at D, tacking down horizontal threads. **(3)** When finished with a row of couching, put ends of horizontal thread in needle and pull through to back side of fabric. **(4)** Couching can be worked in rows as in 3 or in a wheel as in 4.

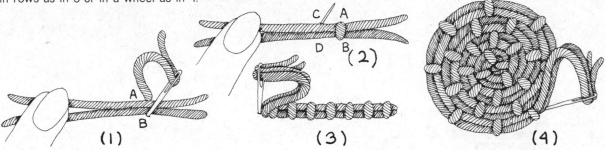

Cross stitch. **(1)** Come up at A; go in at B; go up at C and in at D. Continue across, keeping the needle vertical and spacing the stitches evenly. It helps to count threads or to rule two light lines in pencil as guides. **(2)** To complete the other half of each cross, start from the opposite end and return along the same line of stitches. Again, keep the needle vertical. Go into the same holes worked in the first row of stitches. (You may have to turn the embroidery upside down to accomplish this.)

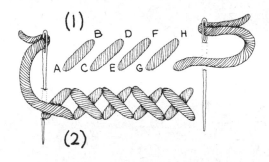

Feather stitch. Come up at A, forming a shallow loop. Hold down with thumb and go in at B. Come up at C, form a loop, hold with thumb, and go in at D. Continue, alternating loops from left to right.

Fishbone stitch. **(1)** Draw a guide line down center of area to be filled. Come up at A at top of guide line. Go in at B, directly below A. Come up at C to left and below A, touching it. **(2)** Go in at D to right and below A, also touching it. Come up at B and form a loop by holding thread under needle. Pull through (not taut). **(3)** Go in again at E, below B, up at F to the left, and below C, touching it. **(4)** Repeat steps 2 and 3 again until the guide line is covered.

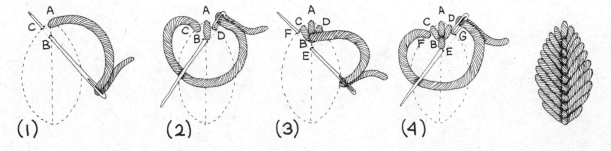

French knots. (1) Come up at A. Hold needle close to fabric and coil thread snugly around needle two or three times. (2) Insert needle at B, very close to A but not in the same hole, meanwhile keeping thread taut with fingers of free hand. More precise but smaller knots can be made by coiling the thread only once around the needle.

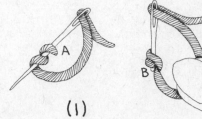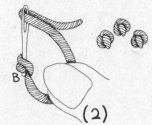

(1) (2)

French knots on stalks. Come up at A, pull thread away from A about ¼ inch, twist thread around needle, and hold taut with free hand. Go in at B. Pull gently through. French knots can be made in rows or in a sunburst shape as shown.

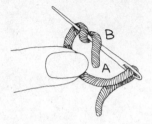

Herringbone stitch. (1) Come up at A; go in at B, diagonally below A. (2) Come up at C, level with B. Cross over last stitch and go in at D, level with A. (3) Come up at E, level with D; go in at F, level with C and B. (4) Repeat steps 2 and 3.

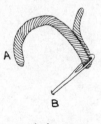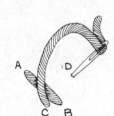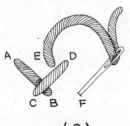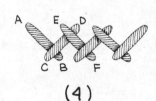

(1) (2) (3) (4)

Close herringbone stitch. (1) Come up at A; go in at B. (2) Come up at C directly below A; go in at D directly above B. (3) Come up at E, next to A; go in at F, next to B. (4) Come up at G, next to C; go in at H, next to D. Continue across to fill in entire area, being careful not to pull thread taut. When covering previous crosses, go into the same hole as you did with the old stitch.

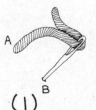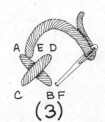

(1) (2) (3) (4)

Laid work held with cross bars. (1) Come up at A; go in at B across top (or widest part) of shape to be filled. Come up at C (just below B) and go across to D. (2) Continue filling area with parallel horizontal lines. Stitches should be close together with no fabric showing between them. (3) Come up at E (at broadest part of shape) and go in at F, laying thread across horizontal threads at about a 45-degree angle. (4) Come up at G about ½ inch from F. Go in at H, keeping thread parallel to EF thread. Continue, covering whole shape with diagonal lines parallel to EF. Repeat from opposite direction to cross these diagonal lines. (5) To hold threads down, come up at I and go in at J. Continue, tying each intersection of horizontal and diagonal threads with a small stitch.

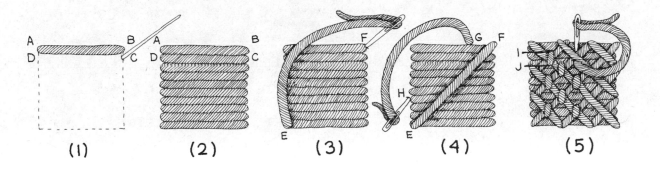

(1)   (2)   (3)   (4)   (5)

Lazy daisy stitch. (1) Bring needle up at A (center of the "daisy"); make a loop with thread and hold down. Go in at B, next to A, and come out again at C. Draw needle and thread over loop and tie down with tiny stitch at D. (2) Continue around circle.

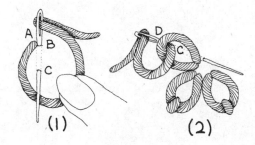

(1)   (2)

Long and short stitch, shaded. (1) Work a row of split stitch along outline of area to be covered. Come up at A and go in at B *over* split stitch. Come up at C and go in at D. CD should be 1½ times the length of AB. (2) In a darker shade of the same color, come up at E, splitting through the end of the first stitch in row 1. Go in at F. Repeat for remaining stitches in row. All stitches in this and succeeding rows are the same length; however, they fit (brick fashion) into the row before. (3) In the darkest shade, work a third row of stitches, always coming up slightly through the ends of the stitches in the previous row.

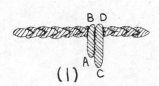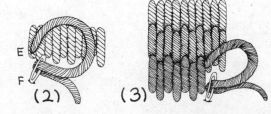

(1)   (2)   (3)

Pekinese stitch. **(1)** Work a line of backstitch. Using a blunt needle, come up at A, just below first backstitch. Push needle through second backstitch (not through fabric) from B to C, leaving a small loop of thread. **(2)** Push needle through first backstitch from D to E, bringing needle out on top of loop made by the first stitch. **(3)** Continue from F to G, leaving a loop as in step 2. **(4)** Push needle through the second backstitch from D to E. Bring needle out on top of loop. Continue to end of row of backstitches.

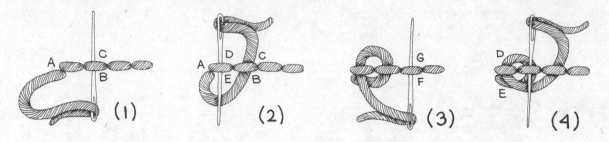

(1)   (2)   (3)   (4)

Running stitch. Come up at A, go in at B, and come up at C. Stitches should be evenly spaced.

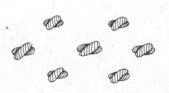

Satin stitch. Come up at A; go in at B. Come up again very close to A and go in close to B, keeping the stitches even and smooth. An outline of split stitches will keep the shape smooth and give a slightly raised edge.

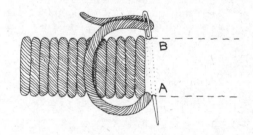

Seeding. **(1)** Come up at A and go in at B a small distance away. Pull through. **(2)** Come up at C; go in at D, diagonally across AB. Pull through. This will form a raised, bump-like stitch.

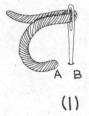 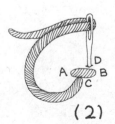

(1)   (2)

Shisha stitch. (1) Hold mirror or other round object in place. To tack down, come up at A close to edge of mirror; go in at B close to other edge. Come up at C; go in at D. Come up at E and go in at F; come up at G and go in at H. (2) Repeat around circle, going from I to J, K to L, M to N, O to P, making another square diagonally on top of the first square of stitches. (3) Come up at A-1; slide needle under threads GH and MN at B-1. Holding thread under needle as shown, draw tight. (4) Take a small stitch in fabric (C-1 to D-1). Loop thread under needle; pull tight. (5) Repeat 4, slipping needle *under* threads GH and MN from squares and *over* thread from the needle. (6) Repeat 4, going into the same hole as with D-1. Come up at F-1 with thread under the needle. Continue around the circle, gradually encasing and pulling back all crossed threads covering the surface of the mirror.

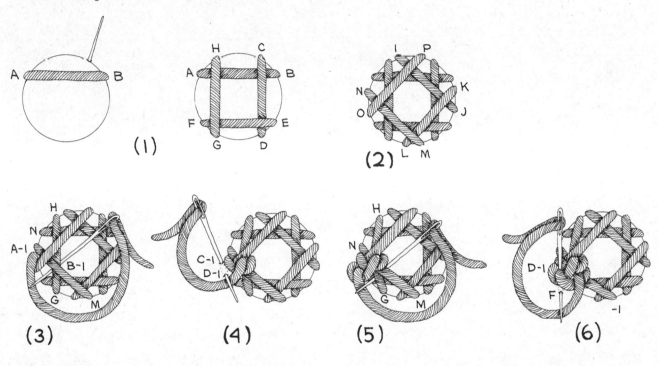

Spider's web. (1) Come up at A and go in at B. Come up at C; go in at D. Come up at E and go in at F; come up at G and go in at H. (2) Come up at I in the center; go under AB and GH. (3) Pull thread through. Go over GH and then under GH and CD. (4) Continue this way, going over one and under two threads until entire web is filled.

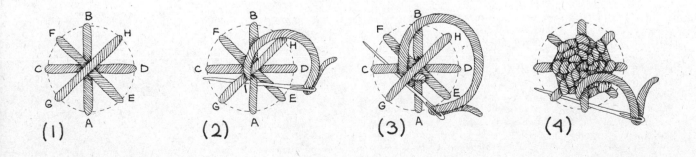

Spiral stitch. This stitch is actually two rows of blanket stitch slanted slightly, with the two rows facing each other. The two rows are done from opposite directions. (See blanket stitch, page 16.)

Split stitch. (1) Come up at A; go in at B. (2) Come up at C. Pierce through center of stitch, splitting it in the middle. (3) Needle goes in at D, a little ahead of B. Repeat to end of row.

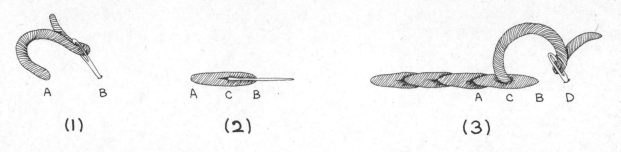

(1)   (2)   (3)

Stem stitch. (1) Come up at A, go in at B, and come up again at C, halfway between A and B. Draw through, holding thread to left of needle. (2) Needle goes in at D and out at the same hole as B. Draw through, keeping thread to left. (3) Repeat step 2.

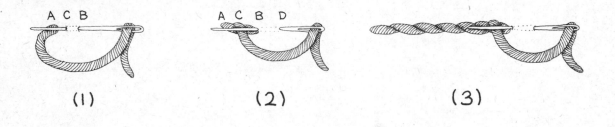

(1)   (2)   (3)

Wave stitch. (1) Come up at A, go in at B, and continue across to make a row of straight stitches. (2) Come up at C below and to the right of A. Slip the needle behind stitch AB without going through the fabric. (3) Go in at D (through fabric) in line with C. Come out at E, next to D, taking only a very small stitch. Slide through next straight stitch above (as in step 2). Repeat to the end of straight stitches. (4) Come up at F below and to the right of C. Slip needle behind C. (5) Go in at G, come out at H, taking a small stitch. Slip needle behind D and E. Continue to the end of row. Rows will grow progressively longer as you work. To decrease, skip the first end and begin to make loops around the next pair of ends.

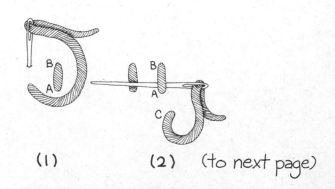

(1)   (2)   (to next page)

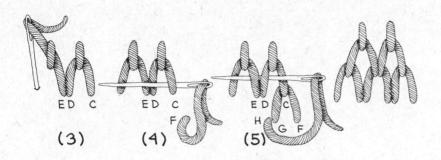

E D C	E D C	E D C		
	F	H G F		
(3)	**(4)**	**(5)**		

Weaving stitch. (1) Make a row of evenly spaced threads A to B, C to D, E to F, G to H, I to J, K to L, and so on. (2) Using a blunt needle, come up at M. Weave under and over. Go in at N. (3) Come up at O, weave across to P, and go in. Come up at Q and continue back and forth until upper area is filled. Then fill in lower half, starting just below M.

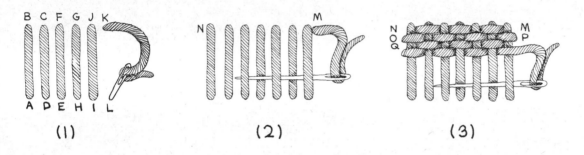

B C F G J K	N ... M	N O Q ... M P
A D E H I L		
(1)	**(2)**	**(3)**

Zigzag braid. (1) Draw three parallel lines. Come up at A a little to the right of center line. Make a loop to the left; hold with thumb. Go in at B on the center line above A. Come out at C through loop on the left line, across from and a little lower than A (see drawing, step 1). Pull through. (2) Insert needle at D to the right of B and above A. Form a loop to the right. Come up at E on the right line (¼ inch lower than C) and pull needle through the loop (see diagram for correct loop placement). From now on, each loop will be about ¼ inch lower than the last loop on the same side. (3) Insert needle at F, just above CE thread, and make a loop to the left. Come out at G, ¼ inch below C and through loop. Pull through. (4) Insert needle at H above EG thread, coming out at I, and continue from left to right, going back to the center line just above the last loop. Repeat. Do not pull the thread too taut. For a more pronounced effect, use a double thickness of thread.

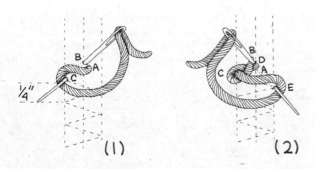

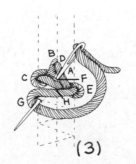

(1)   (2)   (3)   (4)

Machine embroidery

An exciting form of stitchery, machine embroidery may be a completely new medium to you, but if you're used to working with a sewing machine, you'll have no trouble mastering it. Machine embroidery is fast and gives tremendous freedom and very immediate rewards. It also provides unique textures that cannot be achieved by hand.

There are several types of machine embroidery: straight stitching with the presser foot *on* the machine, zigzag and programmed stitches, and free motion embroidery with the foot *off* the machine (the apron project on page 53 was done by this method).

Know your machine

Make friends with your sewing machine. Re-read the instruction manual or take a brush-up course at your sewing machine dealer. It will refresh your memory concerning the special effects your machine can accomplish, its idiosyncrasies, and necessary cleaning and oiling techniques. Pamper your machine; it will work better and last longer. Don't be afraid to play with the upper tension; many unusual effects can be obtained by loosening and tightening it. In general, embroidery requires a tension slightly looser than normal.

Set aside some time to try out some of the stitching techniques described in the machine's instruction manual and those shown in the photo on page 27. Experiment on different scraps of fabric to see what your machine can do.

Cleaning. Review your manual for information on how much cleaning you can do. Use a small brush and a pair of long-nosed tweezers (purchased in hobby shops and scientific supply stores) to remove dust, thread, and lint.

Oiling. Again, refer to your instructional manual for specific information. After oiling, sew several rows of stitches on a scrap of absorbent cloth to blot up any excess oil.

What your machine can do

Don't despair if you don't have a zigzag machine. Lines 1 through 8 on the sampler shown at far right were done with a straight stitch machine, whereas lines 9 and 10 and lines 14 through 17 were sewn with a basic zigzag machine. Lines 11 through 13 are the result of cam attachments used on a deluxe zigzag machine.

Straight stitch machine. By varying threads and adjusting the machine's tension, you can achieve many unusual effects. Although it's more difficult with a straight stitch machine than with a zigzag, some free motion embroidery can be done with the presser foot off the machine. Machine-embroidered Mexican blouses and dresses are done with straight stitch treadle sewing machines.

Zigzag machine. Not only can you do zigzag stitching on this machine but also you can sew satin stitch and its many variations, basic straight stitches, and all free-form embroidery. Some zigzag machines can also take double needles (see rows 14 and 15 on the sampler at right).

Deluxe zigzag machine. In addition to the stitches done by the other machines, each deluxe zigzag has its own built-in programmed stitches, called cams.

Supplies

Organize your sewing area so your supplies (particularly threads) will be easily accessible when you begin work.

Needles. Sharp, new needles in the proper size for the fabric and thread you'll be using are extremely important for successful embroidering. The finer the fabric you use, the smaller the needle's number: numbers 11 American and 70 Continental are the finest sizes; numbers 12 to 14 American and 80 Continental are medium weight; numbers 16 American and 90 Continental are heavy. This numbering system is different from the numbering system for hand sewing needles; on those, the smaller the number, the larger the needle. On machine needles, the smaller the number, the smaller the needle.

Thread. Although machine embroidery thread (sizes 30 and 50) is imported and hard to find, some fabric shops do carry it. You can also use any thickness of normal sewing thread; for special effects, you can wind metallic thread, pearl cotton, or floss on the bobbin. In order for the thicker thread to appear on the right side of the fabric, sew with this side face *down*. If you can fit thick thread through needle's eye, you can also stitch it on top of the fabric. But the top tension may have to be loosened. As each machine's tension is individual, you'll have to play with it to get the desired effect.

Embroidery hoop. Although difficult to find, special machine embroidery hoops are available. They are very shallow and have a half moon cut-out on one side to allow the presser foot to pass over the hoop. These hoops will slide easily under the needle of most machines. If you wish to use a regular wooden embroidery hoop in place of the machine hoop, remove the presser foot. Use a file to remove a small half moon from the rim of the hoop (similar to that found on the machine embroidery hoop). This part of the hoop will be shallow enough to slide under the needle. To get the fabric to lie flat on the machine, turn the hoop upside down, the inside hoop face up.

Scissors. Small, sharp embroidery or cuticle scissors are invaluable for cutting appliques and snipping threads.

Straight stitches

The following straight stitch techniques (as seen at right) are all worked with the presser foot on the machine and can be done with any kind of sewing machine.

Tuck. To make a tuck (line 4), press and pin the tuck into the desired width. Stitch and press again.

Trapunto. Sew two layers of fabric together with two parallel rows of straight stitch following any design. To achieve a corded effect (line 5), thread the yarn or cording through this "tunnel." Or stitch one line, then put cording between the two layers of fabric close to the first line of stitching. Pin in place and then sew the second line of stitching, using a zipper foot instead of a regular presser foot. Sharp curves are best done by the first method.

Metallic and thick threads. Wind the novelty thread on the bobbin by hand, slightly loosening the tension screw on the bobbin case until the thread can run through it easily. Stitch with your fabric *face down* so the bobbin thread will be on the right side of the fabric (line 1).

Before loosening the bobbin tension, make a small scratch or daub a small dot of nail polish on the tension screw to mark its normal placement. Remember: when loosening or tightening anything—left is loose and right is tight.

Quilting. Pin or baste two layers of fabric securely together with padding in between; with a darning foot, sew around a pencilled outline or around the designs already imprinted on the fabric. Secure pinning or basting will prevent puckering. You can use a quilting foot (with a gauge to keep stitches parallel) to do regular diamond-shaped quilting (line 6). To keep stitches from pulling out, backstitch after the first few stitches each time you begin and again at the end of each row of stitching.

Yarn tacking. Sew neatly along one edge of the yarn, slightly stretching it as you go (line 7). Tacked down in this way, the yarn will spring back and stand up on the fabric, hiding the stitching. Sew very close to the edge of the yarn; a zipper foot would be helpful here. Some sewing machine companies make a special foot for this purpose. It has a wide groove (¼-inch wide) on the underside of the foot that guides the yarn through and under the needle without binding or stretching the yarn.

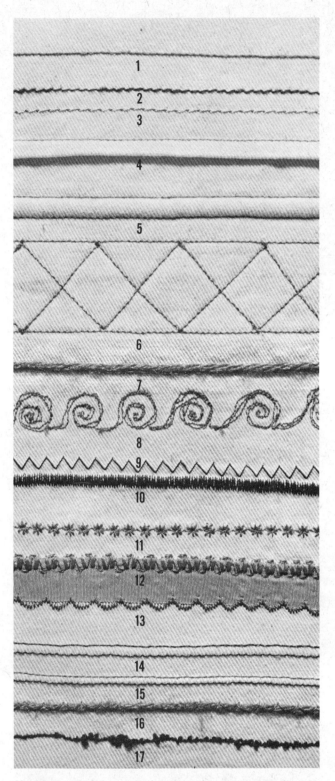

Machine embroidery can be done in many ways (top to bottom): 1) embroidery floss on bobbin (work done face down); 2) thin yarn on top (work done face up); 3) silk buttonhole twist on top; 4) fabric tuck; 5) trapunto; 6) quilting; 7) yarn tacked down with straight stitches; 8) free motion stitching; 9) zigzag; 10) satin stitch; 11) cam; 12) and 13) cam stitches holding down seam binding; 14) and 15) twin needles; 16) yarn held with zigzag; and 17) corded stitch.

Zigzag and programmed stitches

Besides doing rows and rows of decorative stitches—such as satin stitch and tiny ducks and flowers—your zigzag or cam machine can accomplish many interesting techniques. Before embroidering on your project, study your instruction manual and practice some of the special techniques that your machine can do:

Satin stitch. Used for applique, satin stitching is done with a short stitch length and a medium or wide width, depending on the effect desired (line 10). To help the fabric move along easily, lighten pressure on the presser foot. If your fabric puckers, put newspaper or tissue paper strips under the fabric; tear it away afterwards. Use programmed stitches to outline and emphasize areas, to hold tucks decoratively, and to applique. Decorative stitches are particularly effective when used for tacking down or bordering rows of seam binding, ribbon, braid, and narrow lace. Paste, purchased bonding material, or plastic bags can be used to hold the applique in place while working on it. See "Hand and Machine Applique," pages 30 to 33, for more information on these techniques.

Twin needles. Some zigzag machines can use twin needles and two spools of thread. In tucking and straight stitching, you can use one or two colors of thread for interesting effects (lines 14 & 15). Twin needles are available in two widths.

Couching. Tack down yarn and braid with a row of zigzag stitching, using a cording foot to feed the yarn under the foot (line 16). The special foot described in "Yarn Tacking" above will keep the yarn from getting caught in the machine as it is being sewn down.

Free motion embroidery

The two types of free motion embroidery, satin filling and line drawing, are easily mastered with a little practice. Both use some of the same techniques.

First remove the presser foot and either lower the feed dog or cover it with a darning plate (this prevents the fabric from being pulled into the machine). Some machines are equipped with a lever to lower the feed; other types must be covered. To find out which kind of machine you have, check your manual or consult your sewing machine dealer.

Line drawing

To control the size of each line drawing stitch, set the stitch length and width at zero. Stretch the fabric, right side up, over the large ring of your hoop, slipping the small ring inside (the reverse of the procedure in hand embroidery). Always keep the fabric as taut as possible (see illustration 28-A below).

Place the fabric under the needle, bringing the bobbin thread to the top of the cloth so that both threads are on its surface.

Lower the lever that would normally lower the presser foot. *Always* do this before stitching, for this lever controls the top tension.

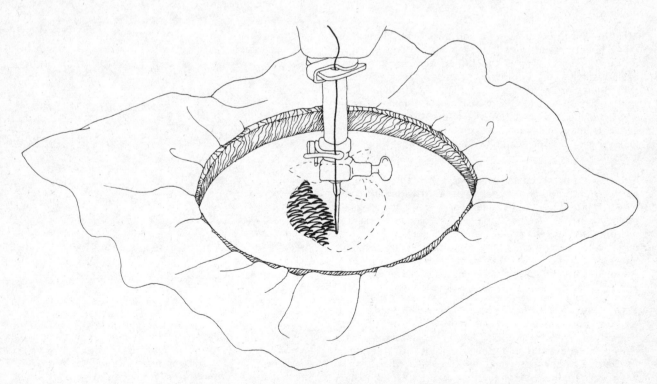

28-A. An embroidery hoop is used differently for machine work than for hand work. Fabric is first stretched right side up over the large ring of the hoop; then the small hoop is pushed down over the fabric and inside the large ring. In effect, you will be working with the hand embroidery hoop upside down, just the opposite of how it is used in hand embroidery.

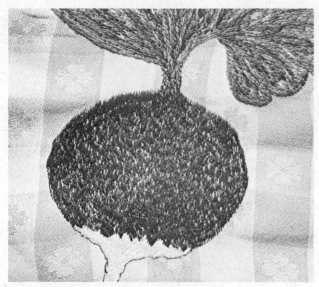

Satin filling technique was used to machine embroider this radish onto a barbecue apron (*see page 50*). *Line drawing technique outlines white root area.*

Start the machine and begin moving the hoop to the left and right, forward and back. Try writing your name or outlining a shape; you'll see how easy it is.

Keep your elbows down and *relax*. Hold the hoop with the thumb and little finger of each hand, keeping your other fingers just inside the hoop but away from the needle. Since the needle is unprotected, remove the fabric and hoop carefully when you have finished.

You can do a corded stitch by loosening the bobbin tension and tightening the top tension. The bobbin thread will come to the surface. By tightening the top tension even more, you will produce a more exaggerated effect. You can achieve a very loopy effect with pearl cotton or floss by loosening the bobbin tension even more and, at the same time, tightening the top tension. Wind the floss on the bobbin by hand. Then move the hoop *slowly* so the loops of bobbin thread will build up. This should be done with the right side of the fabric facing up. Both of these stitches (corded and loopy corded) should be practiced first. Some machines will pull the bobbin thread through the fabric and some won't. The density of the fabric is also a determining factor. Practice to see whether it works better with the right side of the fabric facing up or down on your machine. See page 27, (line 17).

Satin filling

Requiring a little more practice than line drawing, satin filling produces a rich, full effect and is particularly useful for filling in areas of flower petals and leaves. The giant radish decorating the apron shown above and on page 53 was done by this method.

As machine embroidery thread is fine and glossy, but difficult to find, you can use regular cotton or polyester thread in its place.

Following are some satin filling techniques:

Remove the presser foot, lower or cover the feed dogs, and put the fabric in a hoop (as taut as possible).

Set the stitch length at zero, the width at its *widest* setting. Place the fabric under the needle and lower the presser foot lever to engage the top tension.

Now loosen the top tension lever. The top tension should probably be set at zero. Try this and make adjustments as necessary. It must be much looser than the bottom tension so the bobbin thread will actually pull the top thread below to the back side of the fabric.

Keep your elbows flat on the table and your fingers on the hoop and close to the needle (as shown in 29-A, below). Start the machine and move the fabric from side to side and slightly forward with each swing until the area to be filled is covered with horizontal lines. Practice stitching until you find your most comfortable speed; most machines work better at a faster speed. Let the zigzag motion of the machine do most of the work for you.

You may overlap stitches and go back to cover open areas, but it's best to blend areas evenly, as you would with a crayon on paper. Since the same color thread can look quite different at various angles, practice filling in at different directions. Remember that the thread will be going down horizontally—that is, parallel to the front of the machine. If you plan to make the radish on page 51, follow the arrows on the radish pattern for the correct stitch direction.

To fill in an object, such as a leaf or petal, copy the grain lines of a real leaf or petal, outlining its shape in a shade darker than its actual color. This will define it and give it dimension.

To outline areas, move the stitch width to zero. This will produce a straight but slightly tighter stitch than the line drawing stitch given previously. Do the small areas last, if necessary narrowing the stitch width for a neater job.

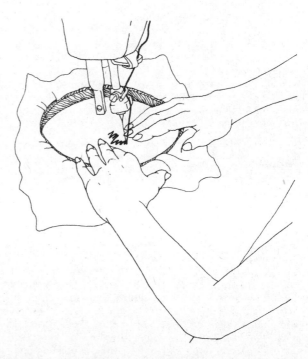

29-A. Good results in machine embroidery are achieved by keeping elbows flat on the table with fingers holding down fabric and thumbs guiding the hoop.

Hand and machine applique

Applique is the art of applying one fabric on top of another to produce bold patches of color. Mastered by South American, Indian, Hawaiian, and African textile artisans, it is probably the oldest and most common form of fabric decoration in existence.

Types of Applique

There are many ways of applying colorful shapes to a background fabric, as shown in illustration 30-A at the right. In *turned* or *blind applique*, the edges of the design are turned under and sewn down invisibly or with decorative stitches; in *stuffed applique*, batting is stuffed under each appliqued piece to raise it up and make it puffy. A *three-dimensional applique* is partially attached to the background fabric but has certain areas which are backed and hang free; an *iron-on applique* is made from commercially available patch kits for clothing repair or from a bonding material placed between two fabrics and melted into the cloth layers by a hot iron. In *Hawaiian applique*, one large motif is used as an overall design; in *layered* or *reverse applique*, several layers of fabric in different colors are sandwiched together and then cut through to the color desired, turned, and sewn down to create a pattern.

All of the applique projects illustrated in this book can be done either by hand or by machine. For examples of hand applique, see pages 57, 60, 64, 66, 67, and 70; for machine applique, see pages 61 and 64.

Supplies

You'll need these basic supplies in your applique work: a #7 or #9 embroidery or millinery needle; 50- or 60-weight thread in a color matching the applique—embroidery floss or pearl cotton can also be used for decorative stitching; sharp embroidery scissors; a thimble (optional); and suitable fabric.

You can use almost any kind of fabric for applique, but non-fraying materials are the best. If you use a loosely woven fabric, back it with iron-on bonding or interfacing to prevent fraying or paint the back with water-diluted white glue. You can back transparent cloth with light-weight interfacing when you stitch it down. Since certain materials, such as felt and leather, are suitable to applique but not to machine washing, determine how you will use the piece before you choose fabrics.

Although felt must be dry cleaned, it is a particularly

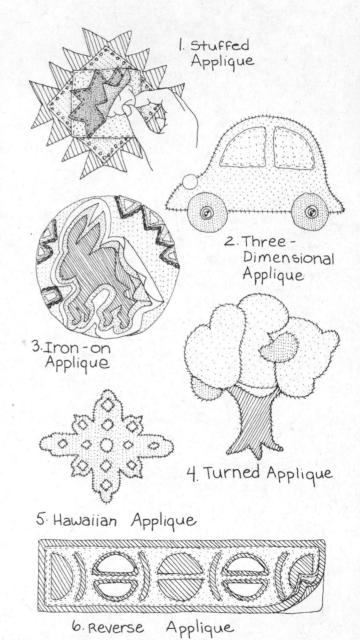

1. Stuffed Applique

2. Three-Dimensional Applique

3. Iron-on Applique

4. Turned Applique

5. Hawaiian Applique

6. Reverse Applique

30-A. Six kinds of applique (top to bottom): **1)** stuffed applique, **2)** three-dimensional applique, **3)** iron-on applique, **4)** turned applique, **5)** Hawaiian, and **6)** reverse applique.

suitable material because you don't have to turn its edges and its stiffness makes it perfect for small pieces with sharp angles and deep curves (see the "Welcome" banner project on page 64).

Follow your own judgment on using a hoop; its function will be to keep your fabric from puckering while you attach appliques.

Because all fabrics have some give, it's best to arrange the grain of the applique so that it runs with the grain of the background fabric to prevent any stretching, tearing, or bubbling of either fabric. Keep this in mind when you are laying out and cutting patterns.

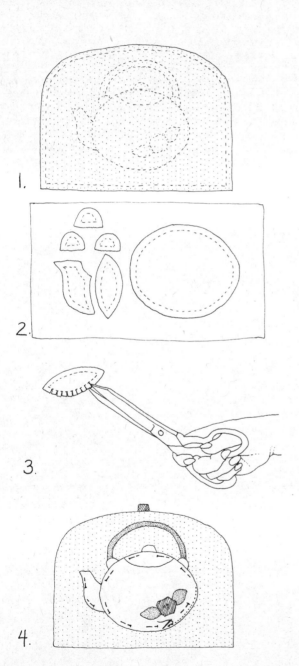

31-A. Steps for applique: **1)** mark background design; **2)** trace patterns and add seams; **3)** cut out patterns, clip seams, and turn edges; **4)** baste in place, then sew.

Making and preparing pattern pieces

Although almost any design can be adapted to applique, start with simple shapes in large sizes. (This doesn't apply to felt, which can be cut easily and doesn't have to be turned under.) Once you have chosen a design, enlarge it to the correct size, adding seam allowances when necessary, and transfer it to your fabric using the instructions on pages 12 to 13. If you plan to repeat the same shape many times, make a cardboard pattern that you can trace.

As shown at left in 31-A, arrange the pattern pieces for your design on the background material. With a semi-hard pencil (use a white-leaded pencil on dark fabrics) trace the outline of each pattern piece onto the background as a guide to follow when attaching the applique. Then trace your patterns onto the applique fabric with a cardboard or paper pattern, leaving enough space around each pattern piece for a 1/4-inch seam if needed.

Cut out the pattern pieces, allowing for seams, and clip any curved or angled areas almost to the pencil line.

Turn under the seam allowance to the pencil line in any of the following ways: lay the pattern over the applique piece on the wrong side of the fabric and iron back all seams around the edges of the pattern; finger press the seam allowance under and baste it with contrasting thread, freeing the edges that will be overlapped by other edges in the design; or pin or partially bond the applique piece to the background and turn under the edges as you work.

The seam allowance on curves should be clipped, eased under gradually, then basted. You can turn under circles by running a thread around the outside edges and gathering it slightly. Then press it flat.

Applique shapes can be attached to fabric either with a turned hem or with decorative hand or machine stitching on the raw edges. Felt and other sturdy fabrics can be left partially uncovered on the edges (see the suede face on the Russian doll, page 67).

Attaching the applique

Before attaching the applique pieces, decide in which order they will be sewn down. Try to position the bottom pieces first, then the middle and top pieces. Pin the appliques in place, giving the arrangement one last check; then baste them down with contrasting thread or pins.

Use a running stitch, whipstitch, buttonhole stitch, or slip stitch to attach the applique to the fabric (see examples on pages 22, 44, 17, and 54). Because each type of stitch will give a distinctive look, decide which effect you'll want. Using a #7 or 8 embroidery or millinery needle, begin stitching along the outline of the piece, using thread in a matching color. For a contrasting effect, embroidery floss and pearl cotton are more effective than regular thread.

When ending or starting a thread, always make knots on the back of the background fabric. When you have finished stitching, remove the basting thread. Then place the piece face down on a padded surface, pressing it gently with a warm iron.

Following are a few tips on handling special problems:

Corners and points. Stitch to within 1/4 inch of the corner or point, backstitch one stitch, and turn the corner under.

Then push the protruding raw edge back under with the tip of your needle and stitch around the corner or point, tucking with the needle tip if necessary. If you are working with acute inside angles, divide the design into several pattern pieces to eliminate the sharp corners.

Floral vines and stems. Use commercially made bias tape for vines and flower stems or cut strips 1¼ inch wide on the bias of a piece of cloth, folding it twice for an overall width of ½ inch. When sewing these strips into curves, sew down the inner part of a curve first and then coax the outer curve into place.

You can achieve a "plaid" effect by weaving together bias tape or ribbon, then stitching it down.

Machine Applique

If you're the kind of person who likes quick results from your work or an end product that can take the wear and tear of constant use, you'll want to use your sewing machine in your applique work. The machine applique projects shown on page 61 were done with a zigzag machine, but by simply adding a seam allowance to each pattern piece and by turning it under, you can topstitch the same designs into place with a straight stitch machine.

Before you begin stitching, refer to your machine's instruction manual for information on machine applique; also refer to the machine embroidery section of this book (pages 26 to 29) for information on zigzag and decorative stitches.

Remember that, although hand stitching will make your appliques puff up, machine stitches will flatten them out.

You can attach applique pieces by machine in one of the ways shown below in 32-A: **1)** Trace your design onto the fabric, adding about ⅛ inch to ¼ inch around the piece when cutting it out. Pin the piece in place on the background and, using a zigzag stitch wide enough to cover the extra fabric allowance, sew the piece down along the edges. **2)** Trace your design onto the fabric, adding 2 inches all around. Pin the piece in place and zigzag along the pencilled outline of the design. When you are finished, carefully clip away the excess cloth with a pair of sharp-pointed scissors. **3)** Trace your design onto the fabric, adding ½-inch seam allowance. Cut out the piece; clip the edges, turning them under. Press the piece. Pin it securely and topstitch it into place with a straight stitch. **4)** Trace the design onto both the fabric and a sheet of iron-on interfacing or a plastic bag. Cut out both pieces and iron the applique and bonding material onto the background fabric. Be sure to cover the fabric with a paper towel or other porous paper when you use a plastic bag. If any plastic leaks out, the paper will blot it and protect the iron plate. Zigzag over the raw edges to finish.

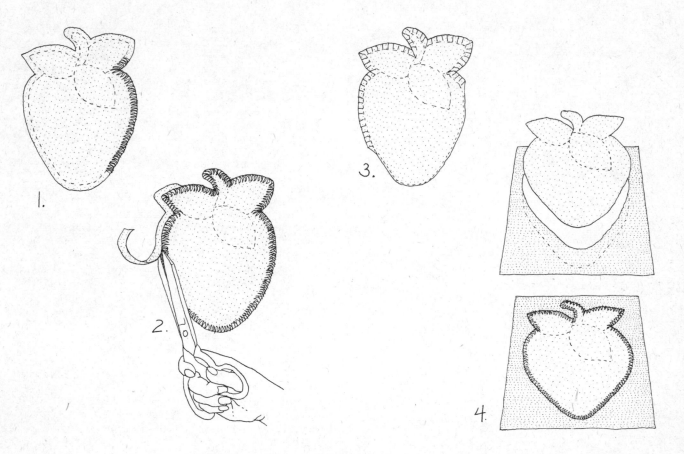

32-A. Four methods of machine applique: **1)** pin fabric to background and zigzag over raw edge; **2)** pin fabric to background and zigzag within seam allowance, removing excess fabric when finished; **3)** clip curves, turn seam allowance under; then top stitch; **4)** fuse fabric to background; then zigzag around raw edges.

Zigzag and straight machine stitches were employed to attach trims, lace, and fabric scraps in shades of pink, red, and pistachio to a background fabric in this picture (detail above). Design: Ann Ammons Bryant. Graphic quality of ''Shooting Star'' (at right) is pointed up by careful use of print fabrics edged with satin machine stitch. Design: Nancy Freeman.

''Foot Stool'' (detail above) contains good examples of machine applique and embroidery. Freeform stitching gives character to applique attachments. For photo showing complete stool, see page 41. Design: Edwina Talley Svoboda. ''Gingerbread House'' (detail at left) shows clever use of plaids, flowered fabrics, lace, and ticking to suggest window panes, bushes, curtains, and shutters. Design: Nancy Freeman.

Finishing, cleaning, and display

Good craftsmanship is just as important in the final stages of stitchery as it is in the beginning. Proper blocking or pressing improves the looks of any piece, and the right kind of framing and hanging will set stitchery off to its fullest advantage.

Blocking, Pressing, and Cleaning

The method you choose to finish your work will depend on the type of fabric and thread you have used for your stitchery or applique. Except for antique pieces or one that is badly puckered or warped, you can block, press, and clean your embroidery at home. When in doubt, take your stitchery to a professional. Consult a yarn shop or dry cleaner for names of professional blockers.

Blocking

Blocking is generally recommended for crewel embroidery and any work done on heavy materials, such as twill or linen, since pressing never quite removes the fine creases and wrinkles in such heavy weaves.

To block your finished work, first snugly cover a piece of fiberboard or soft pine board with a sheet. Soak your embroidery in cold water and lay it down on the sheet while it is still dripping wet. For a smooth, flat finish, lay the embroidery face down; if you want raised and puffy stitches, lay it face up.

Using a T-square or draftsman's triangle as a guide to keep the vertical and horizontal threads of the piece properly aligned, tack its four corners down onto the board with carpet tacks or pushpins (see example at right). Next, pull out the sides of the embroidery, tacking them down at the edges with more tacks. You may have to use pliers to make sure the piece is really taut; the tautness will make it stretch to its correct size and eliminate any puckers and creases that may have developed while it was being stitched on.

For small pieces whose entire embroidered section fits within the confines of an embroidery hoop, follow these directions: pull the fabric as taut as possible in the hoop, making sure the fabric grain is pulled square and not on the bias. Then moisten the whole embroidered area and surrounding fabric with a hand sprinkler or the fine spray of a steam iron. Let the embroidery dry overnight, removing the unwrinkled, unpuckered piece the next day.

Pressing and steaming

Delicate fabrics and threads, such as fine cottons, silks, and metallics, should be pressed or steamed rather than blocked. Applique and clothing decorated with embroidery, such as the examples on pages 64 and 79, can also be finished by pressing or steaming.

Pressing. Pad your ironing board with several thicknesses of terry cloth towels or a soft blanket. This cushion prevents stitches from becoming flattened and keeps their puffy, three-dimensional look.

To finish an embroidery made from washable materials, soak the piece in cold water. While it is still wet, press it face down on the towel or blanket with an iron heated to the appropriate fabric setting. To finish non-washable materials, use the "steaming" method explained below.

Avoid heavy pressing over French knots, bullion stitches, satin stitch, or other raised stitches.

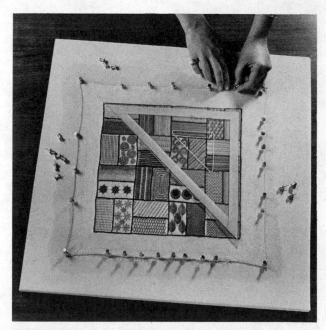

Blocking finished embroidery is easy. Wet the piece; then tack it to a cloth-covered board with push pins. Use a large plastic triangle to keep lines square and at right angles.

Steaming. Steaming can be done with a steam iron or with a dry iron and wet cloth.

If you're using a steam iron, place the stitchery face down on a padded ironing board (see "Pressing," above) and press carefully on the wrong side of the fabric. You can also steam the fabric with the stitchery face up, but be sure to hold the iron *above* the fabric, letting only the steam hit the cloth.

If you're using a dry iron, mount the embroidery in a hoop or stretcher frame (see "Supplies," pages 9 to 11). Then place your iron *upright* on the ironing board (set for linen) and cover it with a wet cloth. Hold the embroidery so the steam can rise through it from underneath; after a short time, the stitches will stand out clearly. (You may want to wear a kitchen oven mitt to protect your hand from the hot steam as shown in the photo below.)

Cleaning

When choosing materials for your stitchery projects, look for washing instructions on the end of the fabric bolt or

Wet cloth draped over dry iron set at highest temperature produces heavy steam to plump up stitches and release wrinkles and puckers from fabric. Wear mitts to protect hands.

on labels attached to yarns and thread. Make a note of these instructions either in your stitchery notebook or on a bulletin board near your washing machine.

Although machine washing is safe for some machine applique and stitchery, it's safer to set your machine for a delicate cycle. If you plan to launder the embroidery by hand, use cool water and pure soap flakes; detergents and bleaches are too strong for delicate hand work. Rinse the embroidery thoroughly in lukewarm water and roll it in a thick towel to blot up excess water. Then hang it to dry.

Wool, linen, and silk should be dry cleaned, but first make sure the shop to which you take your embroidery is reputable and that its personnel have a healthy respect for the hours of work and love you've put into your stitchery.

Framed hangings usually need little care other than an occasional shaking to free dust or a gentle vacuuming with a soft brush attachment.

Framing and Hanging Your Stitchery

Although only a few of the projects in this book require framing and hanging, these tips should help you in future projects as your stitchery talents begin to grow and you move on to other projects on your own. Remember: the design of the frame should complement the stitchery and never overpower it. The stitchery—not the frame—is what's important. The fruit hang-ups on page 61, for example, weren't framed but instead were faced with a matching fabric and hung as is.

In order to make the embroidery fit the frame, many people like to choose a frame before a stitchery is even started. This method works well if you like to plan everything out in advance. But if you like to improvise, changing designs and colors as you go, you'd better wait until the work is finished before you make any decision about framing.

You can gather ideas for framing by visiting art shows and galleries, frame shops, art supply stores, and decorators' showrooms.

Following are suggestions for doing your own framing:

Casings and tubes. This method was used on the banners on page 62. To make a casing, simply hem the top, bottom, and sides of your piece. Felt will need hemming only where the actual casing will be. Cut a dowel or brass rod slightly longer than the width of the hanging, paint or stain it if necessary, and slip it through the casing. The ends of the dowel can be sanded and left uncovered or covered with a tassel or round drawer pull (see the banner on page 64).

Stretcher bars. The sampler on the cover and on page 44 was hung by this method. Stretch the fabric around the bars, being careful to keep the corners as neat and flat as possible, and either staple or tack the fabric to the wood, working from the centers of each side out to the corners. Then staple a piece of sheeting over the back of the frame as a dust barrier.

The sampler on page 78, "Buon Gusto," was framed by this method and then surrounded by a second frame of 1¾ inch redwood strips that were glued at the corners and tacked on with finishing nails. The redwood was then sanded and coated with a sealer.

Primeval plantlife (above), thriving in a surrealistic landscape of deep forest greens and pale blues, is watched over by a burnt orange sun on this hand appliqued quilt done by Jill Friedrick. Simple but sophisticated shapes **(at left),** executed with appliqued lace and Finnish printed fabric in oranges, yellows, and pink on a red background, create a strong graphic statement on this banner. Design: Cathy Lauridsen.

New directions in stitchery

"Jody's Fine Food" (above) brings praise to the cook in hunter green, red-orange, and gold hand-appliqued, stacked felt. Design: Jody House. *"Still Life With Tulips"* **(at right)** incorporates pink, mauve, and peach colored appliqued flowers against a feathery background of embroidered leaves in shades of grey and green. Worked on a quilted velvet panel, this bouquet was designed by Ann Ammons Bryant.

Mistletoe-inspired stitchery (above) is both described and framed by its accompanying woodburned and lettered plaque. This wood and embroidery wall decoration is one of a series based on plant and animal designs. Design: Karen Gray. "Praise the Earth" (**at right**), a hymn to Mother Nature, is sung in shades of blue and mauve. Old velvet and machine satin stitch play a rich accompaniment to the design of this applique banner, made entirely from recycled materials. Design: Barbara Neill.

Bright yellow sun rises over an appliqued and embroidered country scene in "Farm" (**above**). Simple shapes in bright primary colors and floral prints are used to good effect in this picture designed by Irene Peck. "Peaceable Kingdom" (**at left**) is a carnival of gay colors cut into the shapes of birds, animals, insects, flowers, fish, and humans, then appliqued with padding onto a plain white background. The effect is one of joyous merriment. Design: Peggy Moulton.

"Still Life with Apples"(above) employs a child-like purity of pattern against pattern in simple shapes and primary colors accented with a running stitch. Design: Irene Peck. *"A Room . . ."* **(at right)** appears to be awash in a turbulent sea of foamy whitecaps and deep blue water. Strange serpentine shapes undulate below a rippling surface on this applique quilt by Jill Friedrick.

"Aunt Ethel's Front Room" (detail above) recreates with humor a starched and prim sitting room reminiscent of the 1940s. White, candy pink, and pistachio green printed fabrics are cleverly used to simulate wallpaper, curtains, and other furnishings in this quilted and embroidery-trimmed applique picture by Jeanette Kulick. *"Renaissance Doll"* **(at left)** is a three-dimensional stitchery concept using a nylon stocking and batting to create a doll. Inspired by American folk art tradition, the doll is dressed and decorated with hand-stitched clothing and accessories. Design: Ann Ammons Bryant.

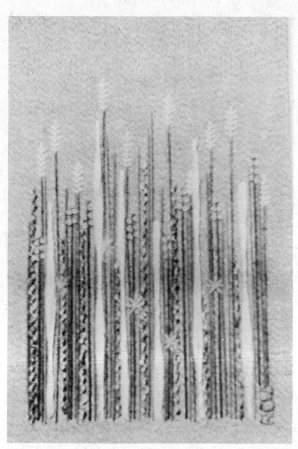

"A Wild Goose Never Laid a Tame Egg" claims this purple and orange applique banner **(above)**. Evidence to that effect can be seen in her wild array of colorful eggs. Design: Sally Paul.

"Marsh Grass" (above) stretches delicately toward the sky in pale pastel shades of pink, yellow, cream, orange, and green embroidery. Design: Roz Shirley.

Imported English Appleton wool is delicately worked on a fine English twill background to create this shy but dutiful little mouse with her broom **(above)**. Design: Marj Gosz. Worked by Natalie Howard.

"We Gather Together" (above) tells a tongue-in-cheek story in tucks, gathers, ridges, and groupings of stitches on a neutral ground of grey and white. Punctuation takes the form of pale pink and navy blue dots, as well as navy blue machine stitching. Design: Doris Hoover.

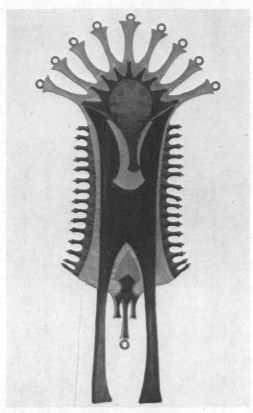

Monolithic hanging (above) resembles ethnic headdress. Machine-appliqued velveteen is stuffed to add dimension. Design: Nancy Gano.

"The Family Hanging" (above) is a modern and humorous translation in stitchery and applique of an old tradition. Design: Peggy Moulton.

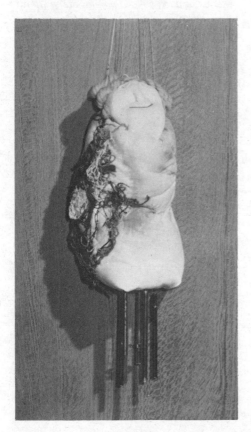

"Elephant Quilt" (detail above) acclaims the gentle pachyderm with sophisticated softness in pale green, yellow, brown, and orange quilted applique. Design: Janny Burghardt. *"Quinella Belle" (at left)* is not only decorative but also functions as a means to call the family together. A delicate set of wind chimes takes the place of her legs. Design: Joan Schulze.

"Foot Stool" (above) is exactly that. Stool is supported by hand-carved legs resembling those in cushion design. Embroidered and appliqued by machine.

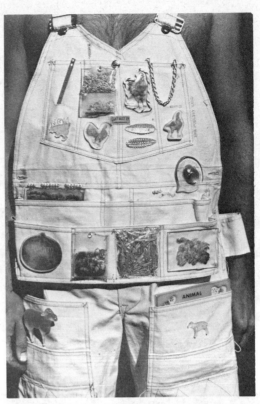

"Homestead Suit" (above) is bemedaled with decals, cast resin animals, beads, and heat-sealed pockets. Design: Margaret Ahrens Sahlstrand.

"Patrick's Dream Bag" (above) is a painted, appliqued, and stitched sleeping bag personalized with the object of Patrick's dreams: a career as a motorcycle daredevil. This stitchery was designed by Gayle Feller.

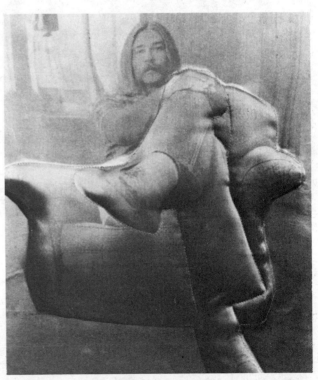

Blueprint on satin creates an ethereal dream-like atmosphere in shades of blue. Hand stitching and padding give dimension to the chair, as well as the legs and feet of the subject. Design: Kay Shuper.

Stitchery projects you can make

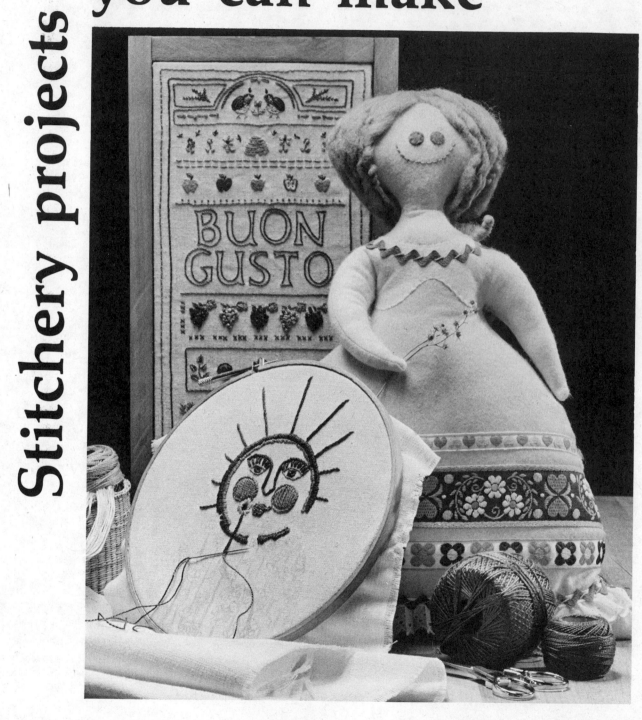

Hopefully by now you're itching to get started on your own stitcheries. The projects on the following pages will enable you to do just that. They are meant to be an introduction to stitchery, teaching you basic techniques and giving you experience with colors, textures, and shapes. They are also meant to tantalize, intrigue, and inspire you, so that, once one project is completed, you'll want to go on to the next and eventually to design and create your own stitcheries.

Make the projects in this book your own. Feel free to improvise: take an embroidery design from one project and use it on another or change colors to suit your needs and color scheme.

The clothing designs on pages 46 to 53 were specifically designed with versatility in mind; for example, the embroidery on the hat shown on page 49 could become a row of flowers marching along the yoke of a shirt or around the hem of a dress. Or one set of large flowers could decorate the tea cosy on page 60.

When substituting colors, you may wish to work a representative part of the design onto a scrap to make sure the colors look well together and achieve the effect you have in mind for your finished project.

Once you've had a little experience with the stitches listed on pages 16 to 25, you'll be able to substitute more difficult or unusual ones for the stitches recommended in the project. The box "Using Stitches" on page 12 can help you decide which stitch substitutions are appropriate.

Above all, remember that there are no strict rules in stitchery. If you use stitches, colors, fabrics, and designs that please you, the finished product will be an exciting, appropriate, and unique creation.

A key to colors and stitches

This master key will indicate letter and number abbreviations for stitches and colors to be used when making the projects on the following pages. These are found on the patterns, as are a series of dots bordering each pattern which, when joined horizontally and vertically, will form a convenient transfer grid (for directions on how to use the grid see pages 12 and 13). The stitches listed below run alphabetically from page 16 to 25.

Stitch Key

A.	Backstitch	Q.	Close herringbone stitch
B.	Blanket stitch	R.	Cross bars over laid work
C.	Brick stitch	S.	Lazy daisy stitch
D.	Bullion knots	T.	Long and short stitch
E.	Buttonhole stitch	U.	Pekinese stitch
F.	Chain of grain	V.	Running stitch
G.	Chain stitch	W.	Satin stitch
H.	Double chain stitch	X.	Seeding
I.	Chevron darning	Y.	Shisha stitch
J.	Couching	Z.	Spider's Web
K.	Cross stitch	AA.	Spiral stitch
L.	Feather stitch	BB.	Split stitch
M.	Fishbone stitch	CC.	Stem stitch
N.	French knots	DD.	Wave stitch
O.	French knots on stalks	EE.	Weaving stitch
P.	Herringbone stitch	FF.	Zigzag stitch

Color Key

1.	light blue	24.	deep gold
2.	medium blue	25.	yellow
3.	dark blue	26.	deep yellow
4.	turquoise blue	27.	red
5.	dark turquoise blue	28.	magenta
6.	light orange	29.	maroon
7.	medium orange	30.	light pink
8.	dark orange	31.	medium pink
9.	burnt orange	32.	deep pink
10.	rust	33.	red orange
11.	peach	34.	purple
12.	light green	35.	deep purple
13.	medium green	36.	lavender
14.	dark green	37.	mauve
15.	bright green	38.	ecru
16.	grey green	39.	grey
17.	dark grey green	40.	dark grey
18.	apple green	41.	white
19.	dark apple green	42.	silver
20.	olive green	43.	light brown
21.	dark blue green	44.	medium brown
22.	light gold	45.	dark brown
23.	gold	46.	black

Sunshine sampler

(Color photo on page 49)

This bright, cheerful sampler can become a large purse or shopping bag. Or it can be stretched over a frame and hung on a wall as a wall decoration, as shown on the cover and on page 49. Either way, this project is like a series of stepping stones along the path to learning 32 different stitches. All stitches are shown and explained on pages 16 to 25.

Materials: You'll need ½ yard off-white linen or other coarsely woven fabric; pearl cotton: one ball each of dark orange, medium orange, gold, and yellow; one ball of medium brown for the outline; four 13-inch stretcher bars (available at art supply stores); 3 shisha mirrors (available at stitchery shops and hobby shops) or substitute cardboard circles (about ¾ inch in diameter) covered with aluminum foil, or 3 pennies; large embroidery needle; embroidery hoop; scissors.

1) Enlarge entire pattern to 12 inches square and transfer to fabric.

2) With the fabric stretched tightly in a hoop, fill in each rectangle, following the color and stitch guides on the pattern. Fill in all the spaces, moving the hoop as necessary. Work the space with the mirrors last, since it may be difficult to reposition your embroidery hoop around them once they have been sewn down.

3) Outline rectangles with rows of chain stitch in medium brown thread.

4) Block or press by any of the methods discussed on pages 34 and 35.

5) Stretch fabric around stretcher bars, tacking or stapling each of the four corners of fabric to the back of the frame. Pull sides of fabric around snugly and tack down between centers and corners.

Two additional finishing stitches

Described here are two stitches used for embellishing or adding finishing touches to stitcheries: the Whip stitch and the Quilt tying stitch.

Whip stitch: thread a #10 sharp needle with thread and, slanting the needle to the left, stitch through both layers of cloth.

Quilt tying stitch: 1) thread a #13 chenille needle with three 12-inch long strands of tapestry wool or pearl cotton and stitch down through all layers of cloth, then up through all layers. 2) and 3) tie a firm square knot and trim yarn ends to even them.

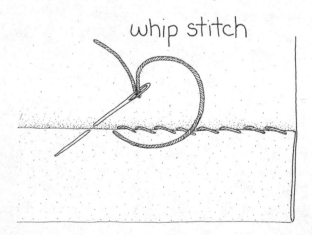

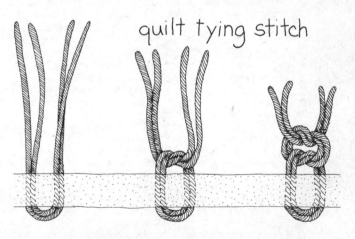

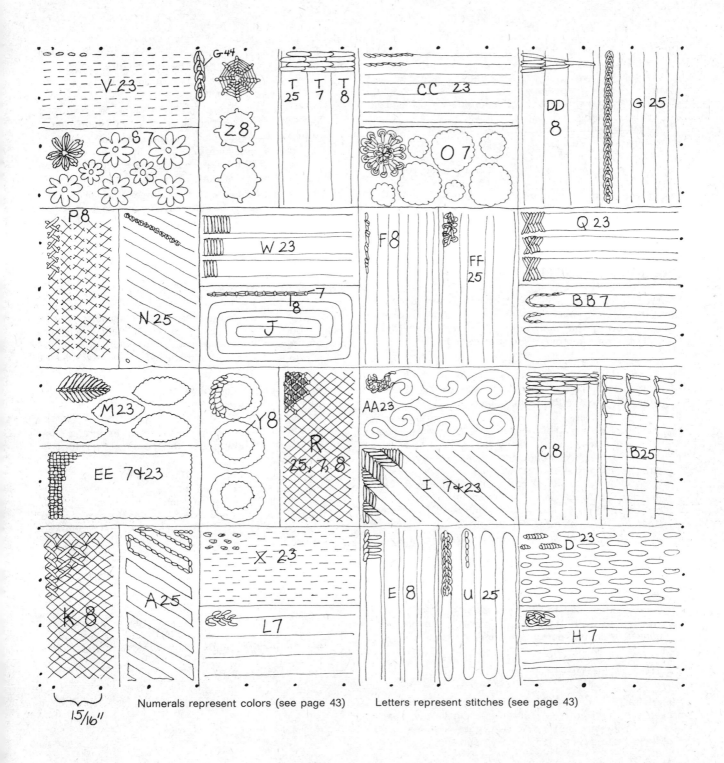

V 23
G 44
S 7
Z 8
T 25
T 7
T 8
CC 23
O 7
DD 8
G 25
P 8
N 25
W 23
J 7 8
F 8
FF 25
Q 23
BB 7
M 23
EE 7&23
Y 8
R 25,7,8
AA 23
I 7&23
C 8
B 25
K 8
A 25
X 23
L 7
E 8
U 25
D 23
H 7

15/16"

Numerals represent colors (see page 43)   Letters represent stitches (see page 43)

A bouquet of patterns

(Color photos on page 49)

The designs shown at right and on page 48 could be used decoratively on garments such as those found on page 49. Planned with versatility in mind, each pattern may be enlarged, reduced, repeated, or cut apart to suit a variety of needs. Though shown as hand embroidery, each could easily be worked in applique or machine embroidery.

Such items as the hat and shoes were embroidered in hand, whereas designs used for larger garments were worked in the hoop. If you plan to make your own ties, transfer the tie pattern onto your fabric first so you will know where to position the design. Then transfer the design and do the embroidery before the tie is cut out.

While several of these patterns are not shown in photographs, each design does have a color key and list of suggested stitches for your convenience.

Blooming Tennis Hat

Materials: Collect 1 skein each of embroidery floss in dark purple, light purple, light yellow, dark yellow, medium orange, apple green, and dark grey green; purchased tennis hat; large embroidery needle; scissors.

1) Enlarge pattern on facing page and transfer to crown of hat. Repeat until all panels are filled. Each single flower should be placed with its center over an eyelet (located in the center of each panel).

2) Don't divide any of the floss, for all six strands will be used for each color. For all flowers, begin by filling in the yellow centers of the large flowers, which should be worked around the eyelet, leaving a hole at its center (see 46-A, below). Next, fill in horizontally the centers of the smaller flowers. All flower petals are then embroidered with satin stitch, following the color key on the pattern. These stitches will all radiate out from the centers of the flowers.

3) With light green floss, fill in stems and petals of each flower with satin stitch. Stitches should be horizontal on all stems, vertical on the leaves of the smaller flowers, and "grow" like veins from the middle of the leaves of the large flowers.

4) Outline petals of large flowers, as well as *all* stems and leaves, with stem stitch, following the pattern color key until all panels are completed.

Embroidered Espadrilles

Materials: Collect 1 skein each of embroidery floss in dark green, medium blue, purple, medium yellow, deep pink, and magenta; 1 pair purchased canvas shoes; embroidery scissors; large embroidery needle.

1) Enlarge pattern on page 48 and transfer it to the top of the shoe and to heel. Repeat on other shoe.

2) Don't divide floss, for all six strands will be used for each color in the design.

3) With a narrow satin stitch, fill in green, blue, and purple rainbow-shaped lines on tops of shoes.

4) With yellow floss, fill in outline of flower design on the face of each shoe with satin stitch. Vary the width of the stitches to fit areas to be filled, with the widest stitches falling between the pink petals.

5) Fill in pink petals and magenta half-circle on each shoe with wide satin stitch to complete each shoe top.

6) Fill in blossom design on each heel (as in steps 4 and 5) with wide satin stitches on magenta and pink areas, varying widths to fill in the yellow outlines.

Sunshine and Flowers Tie

Materials: Gather 1 skein each of embroidery floss in yellow, gold, orange, red orange, red, magenta, lavender, purple, medium blue, dark blue, and medium green; embroidery needle; scissors; purchased tie or materials and commercial tie pattern.

1) Enlarge pattern on page 48 to size indicated and transfer it to a ready-made tie, or fabric for a home-made tie.

2) Divide small batches of floss into three-strand segments. All embroidery on this tie should be done in three-strand floss.

3) For a home-made tie put fabric in a hoop and, following the color and stitch guides on the pattern, fill in the entire design by starting with the smiling sun. Next, work all the floral stems, saving the flower faces themselves for last. Ready-made ties must be worked in hand.

46-A eyelet centers for hat

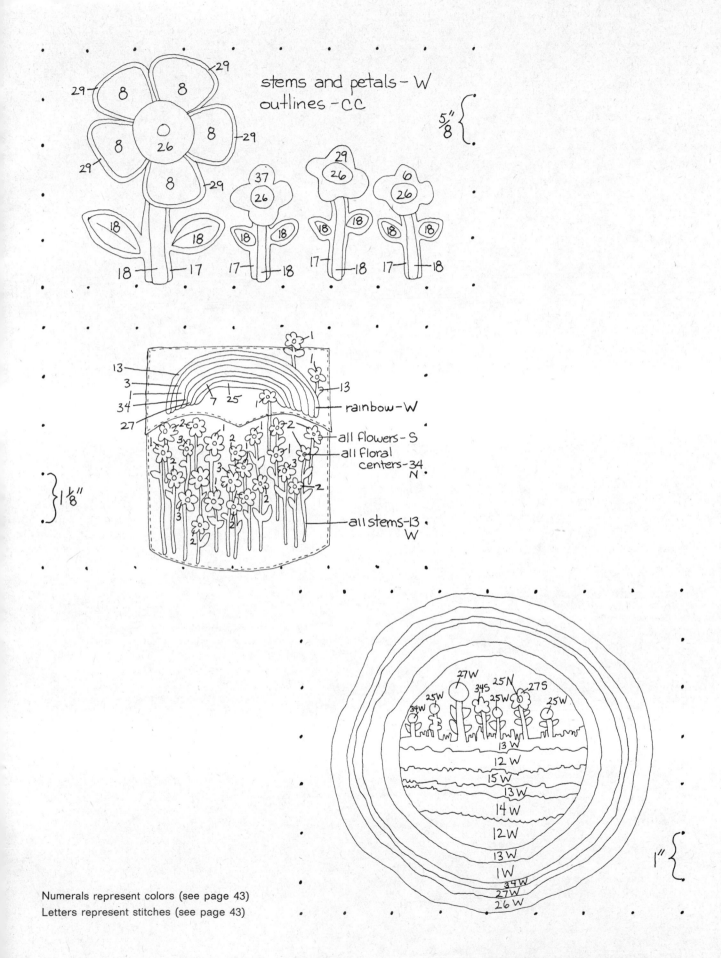

stems and petals - W
outlines - CC

$\frac{5}{8}$"

29 — 8   8 — 29
29   8   26   8   29
29 — 8 — 29

37
26

29
26

6
26

18   18   18   18   18   18   18   18
18 — 17   17 — 18   17 — 18   17 — 18

$1\frac{1}{8}$"

13
3
1
34
27   7   25   1   13

rainbow - W
all flowers - S
all floral centers - 34 N
all stems - 13 W

27W   25N
25W   34S   275
34W   25W   25W   25W

13 W
12 W
15 W
13 W
14 W
12 W
13 W
1W
34W
27W
26 W

1"

Numerals represent colors (see page 43)
Letters represent stitches (see page 43)

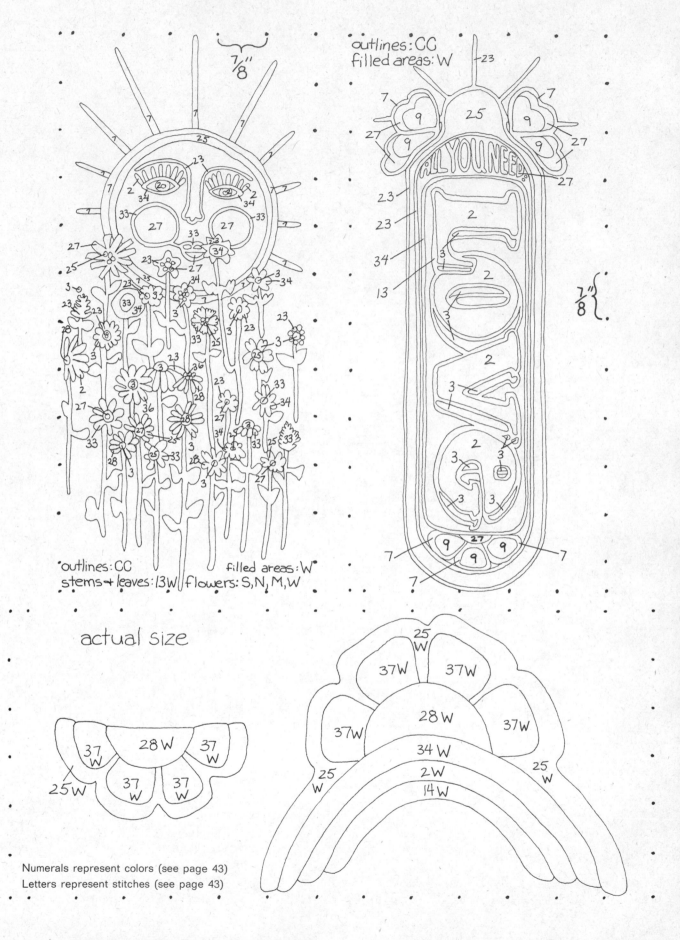

actual size

Numerals represent colors (see page 43)
Letters represent stitches (see page 43)

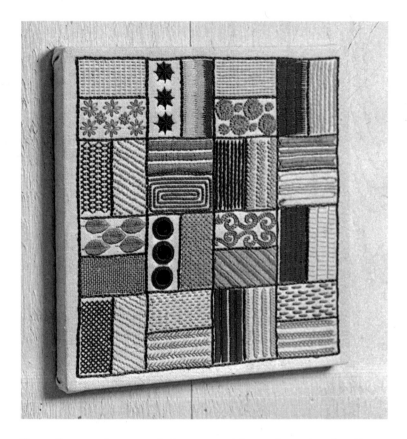

Jaunty espadrilles are real show-offs with their cotton floss embroidered pop-art pansies. Directions begin on page 46. Design: Karen Cummings. Pocket design and Flower Patch design on page 47, and Love tie design on page 48 were also designed by Karen Cummings.

Decorative sampler proves to be ornamental as well as a functional learning tool. Directions begin on page 44. Design: Tina Kauffman.

Add a little garden color to your local tennis court with this multicolored floral-embroidered sun hat. Directions begin on page 46. Design: Karen Cummings.

The sunshine of your favorite guy's life could be this cheery embroidered tie. Directions begin on page 46. Design: Karen Cummings.

Inspirations from Mother Nature

(Color photos on pages 52 and 53)

Lovebirds Peasant Embroidery

An ethnic-inspired design such as this can be used to adorn anything from a caftan to a work shirt or be enlarged and simplified for use as a wall hanging.

The two panels are mirror images of each other; after you transfer one side, turn your pattern paper over to mark the transfer so that the mirror image can be transferred to the other half of your shirt.

Materials: Gather 1 skein each of embroidery floss in yellow, orange, peach, purple, turquoise blue, medium green, and brown; embroidery needle and hoop; scissors; purchased blouse or shirt.

1) Enlarge design and transfer to blouse or shirt.
2) Put area of blouse to be embroidered in a hoop. If necessary, baste a scrap of sturdy fabric to neck opening to make an extension for the hoop to grab.
3) Fill in chain stitch areas first, outlining, then working in to the center of each shape (50-A).
4) Work French knots on orange and blue flowers and in birds' eyes. Use satin stitch for birds' beaks.
5) Outline panel of shirt in green chain stitch.

Chain of Flowers

Springtime blossoms and perky bees decorate the Western-style work shirt shown on page 52. This mixed bouquet would also be at home on a lady's shirtdress or ringing the hem of a child's jumper. The two front yoke designs are mirror images of each other, as are the back yoke designs. The bee can be placed on the back as shown or perhaps on the collar, a pocket flap, or a cuff.

Materials: Collect 2 skeins each of embroidery floss in medium and dark green; and 1 skein each in light green, lavender, purple, light pink, medium pink, yellow, light blue, medium blue, light orange, medium orange, dark orange, black, ecru; embroidery needle and hoop; scissors; purchased shirt.

1) Enlarge and transfer designs to right front and right back yokes of shirt. Reverse designs and transfer them to left front and left back yokes.
2) Divide batches of floss into three-strand segments. All embroidery on this shirt should be done in three-strand floss. To divide floss easily, follow the instructions on page 14.
3) Put shirt in a hoop and fill in areas, either progressing from one color to another or from one stitch to another, following the pattern color and stitch guides.

4) When finished, press, using one of the methods listed on page 35. Launder by hand in warm water.

Super-Radish Apron

Machine embroidery decorates the chef's apron shown on page 53. Satin filling, described on page 28, is fast and easy; it effectively fills in the bright colors. This design would adapt well to machine or hand applique, as well as to hand embroidery.

Materials: Gather one spool each of #50 machine embroidery thread (or substitute with regular sewing thread) in red, white, light green, medium green, and dark green; purchased apron; scissors; zigzag sewing machine; embroidery hoop.

1) Enlarge and transfer design to apron.
2) Refer to section on "Machine Embroidery" (pages 26 to 29) for specific information on machine adjustments; then put fabric in a hoop.
3) Start filling in leaves with medium green thread (bobbin thread can be white). The stitches should be sketched in lightly, running parallel to the length of the leaf. Do not fill the entire leaf.
4) Switch top thread to light green. Sketchily fill in leaves to give a variegated effect. Then outline each leaf with a light green border.
5) With darkest green thread, fill in veins on all three leaves. Stitch top leaf with dark green, lightly filling in entire area to give a three-dimensional effect by making front leaves stand out.
6) Run a few light green and medium green lines into stem.
7) Change to red thread. Outline red area; then fill in with widest zigzag stitch, going the length of the radish.
8) Fill in white root.
9) To outline root with red thread, set machine on straight stitch but do not put on presser foot or change tension.
10) Snip threads and press according to one of the methods discussed on page 34.

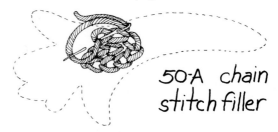

50-A chain stitch filler

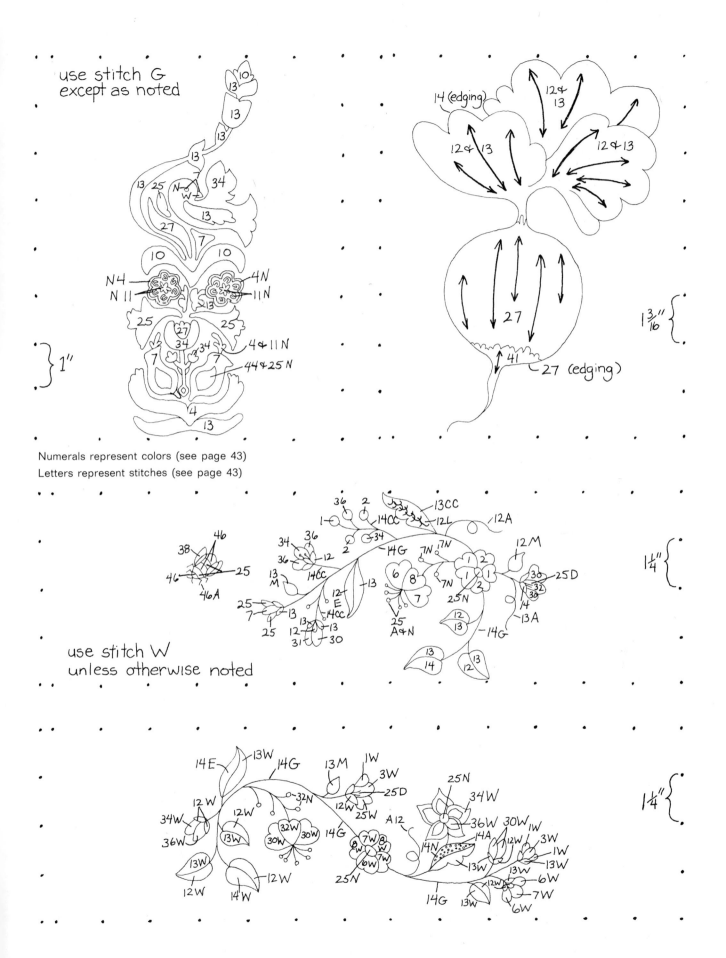

use stitch G
except as noted

10
13
13
13
13
13 25 N 34
W
13
27
7
10   10
N4   4N
N11   11N
13
25   27   25
34
34 34
7   7   4 & 11N
44 & 25N
4
13

14 (edging)   12 &
13
12 & 13   12 & 13

27
41
27 (edging)

1³/₁₆″

1″

Numerals represent colors (see page 43)
Letters represent stitches (see page 43)

36   2
1   14CC   13CC
34 36   12L   12A
2   34
36   12   14G 7N 7N   12M
38   46   14CC   1 2
46   25   13   13   1
46   M   6 8   7N 1 1
46A   25   12 13   7   2   30 25D
7   13   E   25N   32
25   12 13   14CC 25   12 4 30
31   30   A&N   13   13A
13   14G
14   12 13

use stitch W
unless otherwise noted

1¼″

14E   13W 14G   13M 1W
3W
32N   25D
12W   12W 12W
34W   12W   25W A12   34W
36W   13W   32W 30W 14G 14A 25N 36W 30W 1W
30W 30W   7W 8   12W 3W
13W   6W W 14N   1W
12W   12W   25N 6W 7W   13W
14W   14G 13W   12W 6W
13W   7W
6W

1¼″

These Pennsylvania Dutch-inspired lovebirds and flowers lend rustic charm to a cotton dress, peasant blouse or work shirt. Directions begin on page 50. Design: Elissa Hirsh.

Rugged Western work shirt softens to the touch of a profusion of pastel colored flowers, while sprightly bees add a buzz of bright color along the shirt yokes. Photo at left gives a close up view of front yoke design, showing fine embroidery work. Directions begin on page 50. Design: Robin Wagman.

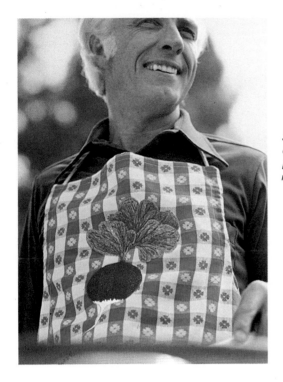

Saucy radish adds a little zest to our chef's table-cloth-check barbecue apron. Machine embroidery produces the tactile, heavily embossed effect of the radish. Directions on page 50. Design: Lynne Morrall.

Richly ornamental crewel work collar has a secret: it began its life as the Underground Sampler discussed on page 7. Persian wool yarn worked on medium weight drapery fabric gives textural interest. Directions begin on page 54. Design: Lynne Morrall.

Crewel collar sampler

(Color photo on page 53)

This Persian wool collar is described as "The Underground Sampler" on page 7. Although it is an unconventional alternative to a traditional sampler, it uses 14 different stitches and serves the same purpose as a traditional sampler. Utilizing a listing of the stitches you've learned, this sampler is an excellent piece on which to practice new stitches as well.

The collar can be worn over a sweater (as shown in the photo on page 53) or attached to a simple V-necked blouse or dress to form a rich-looking, decorative yoke.

Eight vivid colors of Persian yarn are used on a bright green, medium-weight, coarsely woven drapery fabric. Since the collar is symmetrical, each of the shapes and stitches is repeated on the left and right halves of the collar.

Materials: This calls for ½ yard of medium-weight, coarsely woven fabric in bright green (cotton homespun, linen, rayon-linen or rayon-cotton drapery fabric); 3-ply Persian yarn: one small skein each of red, burnt orange, deep purple, dark turquoise, light turquoise, bright green, magenta, lavender; tapestry needle; embroidery hoop; 6 shisha mirrors (available at stitchery shops and hobby shops) or substitute aluminum foil-covered cardboard circles or pennies; sewing needle and bright green thread; ½ yard of light weight backing fabric (bright green or co-ordinating color); large hook and eye; a pair of sharp embroidery scissors.

1) Enlarge pattern and transfer it to fabric, following one of the methods suggested on pages 12 and 13.

2) Do not cut out collar; embroidery will be done first, so that a hoop can be used to keep fabric from puckering. An 18-inch square of fabric will accommodate the pattern and is a comfortable size to work with.

3) Divide batches of yarn into 2-strand segments. This can be done all at once or as you work and change colors.

4) Put fabric in hoop. Following the pattern stitch and color guides, fill in each with the proper stitch. Circles marked "shisha" are for the mirrors; save these for last since it may be difficult to re-position your embroidery hoop around them once they are sewn down.

5) To finish the collar, cut it out, leaving a ½-inch seam allowance all around. Cut out backing fabric to match. Turn under seam allowance on both pieces, pin the wrong sides together, and slip stitch seams shut (see illustration 54-A, below). For a puffy, 3-dimensional effect, stuff collar with dacron or cotton batting before stitching backing to front.

6) Sew on a hook and eye at back of collar.

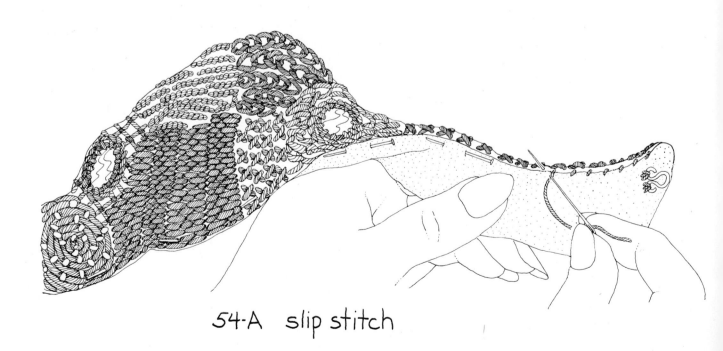

54-A slip stitch

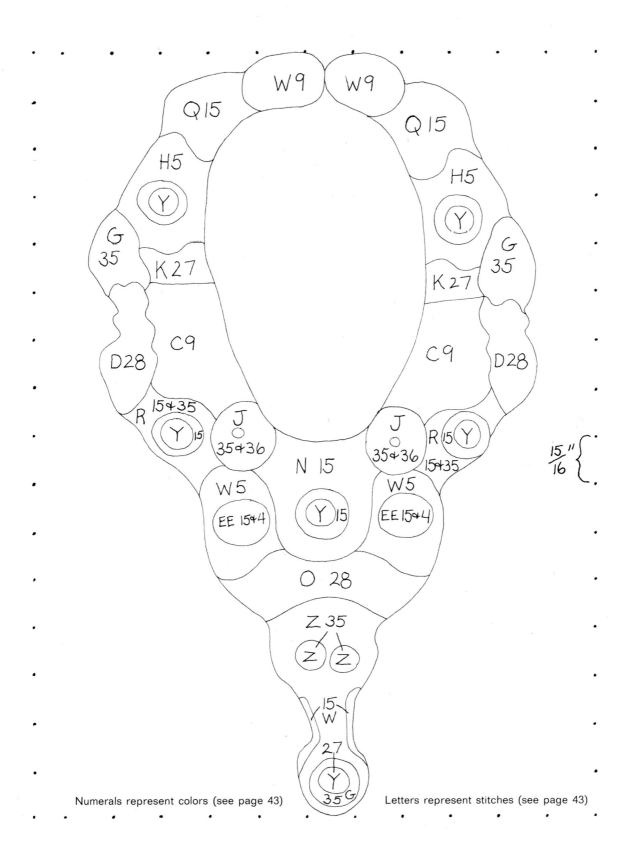

W9   W9

Q15   Q15

H5   H5
Y   Y

G   K27   K27   G
35   35

C9   C9

D28   D28

R 15+35   R 15+35
Y 15   J   J   Y
         O   O
         35+36   N 15   35+36

W5   Y 15   W5
EE 15+4   EE 15+4

O 28

Z 35
Z   Z

15
W
27
Y
35 G

15"
16

Numerals represent colors (see page 43)   Letters represent stitches (see page 43)

Crewel belt buckle

A commercial belt buckle kit is the basis for this crewel-covered buckle. The abstract floral design is done with 2 strands of Persian yarn on coarsely woven fabric.

Materials: Collect 1 belt buckle kit (3″ in diameter); one 9 inch square piece of red, evenly woven, coarse fabric, such as linen, cotton homespun, or synthetic blend drapery fabric; 3-ply Persian yarn, one small skein each: pink, yellow, orange, green, lavender, turquoise, and 2 small skeins of red; #18 tapestry needle; small embroidery hoop; 9 inch square of soft fabric for backing and loop; sewing needle and thread; scissors.

1) Enlarge design and transfer it to fabric.
2) Put fabric in hoop and separate batches of yarn into 2-strand segments.
3) Following color guide, fill in color sections, using the satin stitch. Work from the center out toward edges, building up a new texture on top of the fabric by working stitches as closely together as possible and completely covering the background fabric.
4) Using the paper pattern in the buckle kit as a guide, draw a pencil outline around finished design on back-ground fabric. It will extend ⅛ inch to ¼ inch beyond design all the way around.
5) Zigzag with sewing machine along this pencilled outline to keep fabric from raveling when cut. Cut out fabric according to instructions on buckle kit, except substitute zigzag line for cutting guide. Follow rest of instructions on kit for covering buckle (except for instructions about inside edges since you will be covering the entire face of the buckle).
6) Cut a circle of soft backing fabric slightly larger than the circumference of finished buckle. Clip the edges; then turn them under and slip stitch to back of buckle all the way around (for an illustration of how to do the slip stitch, see page 54).
7) Prepare a 1¼-inch-wide strip of backing fabric, ½-inch longer than diameter of finished buckle, to serve as a loop through which belt will pass in back of buckle. Fold the strip in half lengthwise and stitch down the length of it by machine or hand, taking a ¼-inch seam allowance. Turn strip and press. Turn under ends ¼-inch and slip stitch to fabric edges across middle back of buckle. Belt can then pass through and be fastened with snaps or hooks.

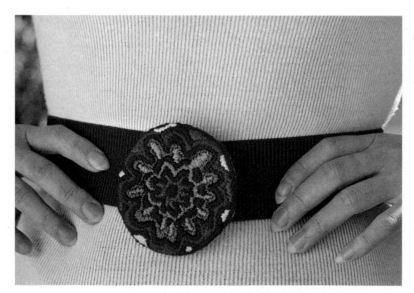

Brilliant, jewel-like colors characterize this crewel covered belt buckle worked over a purchased belt buckle kit. Directions begin above. Design: Marilyn Bauriedel.

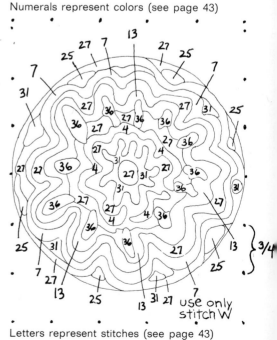

Numerals represent colors (see page 43)

Letters represent stitches (see page 43)

Reverse applique belt

Reverse applique, a technique perfected by the San Blas Indians, was the inspiration for this belt. Three colors of 100% cotton fabric are layered and then trimmed back and sewn down, revealing areas of yellow and black.

Materials: You'll want ¼-yard each of 100% cotton untreated (not permanent press) fabric (synthetic and treated fabrics fray easily and do not hold a crease) in red, black, and yellow; 25½ inches of 3-inch wide buckram or *heavy* interfacing; red and black sewing thread; #9 or 10 millinery needle; grommet maker and 4 brass-colored grommets; 2 yards of red leather or suede lacing; sharp scissors; sewing machine; iron.

1) Cut red, yellow, and black rectangles, each 25½ inches by 3 inches. For backing, cut a second black rectangle 26½ inches by 4 inches.

2) Enlarge design (below right) and transfer it to red fabric, following illustration 57-A.

3) Place yellow fabric on the bottom, black in the middle, and red on top; then pin all three together.

4) By machine or hand, baste both horizontally and vertically between crescent shapes and around all edges.

5) Press with a warm iron. Then, with very sharp small scissors, cut out a red layer on first crescent about ⅛-inch *inside* of its transferred outline. This ⅛-inch will give a seam allowance to be turned under. When cutting, be very careful not to cut black and yellow layers. Round out corners if necessary; curves are easier to turn and tack down.

6) Fold red fabric under ⅛-inch and sew down with a very fine backstitch. When you get to the rounded corners, use your needle point to push fabric under.

7) Continue cutting and turning under crescent edges of the top (red) layer. Only remove basting threads that are in your way; leave as much in as possible until you have tacked all the raw edges down.

8) Continue cutting and turning, moving on to black and yellow layers, until all crescents are completed.

9) On sewing machine, baste ¼-inch in from all 4 edges; then press. Trim to even up all the edges.

10) Cut out buckram to face belt; then lay belt on top of buckram and previously cut black backing fabric.

11) Fold long top and bottom edges of backing over twice to meet basting line. Pin. Slip stitch (see page 54) to front of belt. Fold over side edges twice. Pin and slip stitch. Press and remove basting thread.

12) Put in grommets; then thread a folded, ½-yard length of lacing through each grommet and secure with a slip knot.

Numerals represent colors (see page 43)

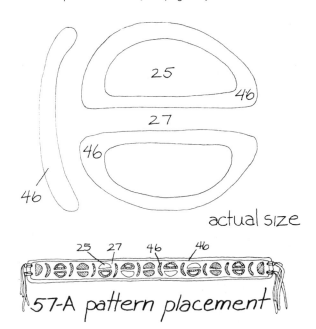

San Blas-inspired reverse applique belt makes good use of repeated design element in three snappy colors. Directions begin above. Design: Sachi Honmyo.

Kitchen applique

(Color photos on pages 60 and 61)

The designs shown here and on pages 60 and 61 are applique ideas that could be done by hand or by machine.

Any tea drinker would appreciate a cheerful appliqued and quilted tea cosy shown on page 60. A double thickness of dacron batting assures that cosy-covered tea will stay hot for at least several hours.

The flying fish hot pad shown on page 61 is done by machine applique. Made with leftover sewing scraps in complementary colors, it is padded with cotton batting (which does not conduct heat) or an old potholder.

Not shown in color, the "Home Sweet Home" design on page 61 could be executed from sewing scraps in bright, provincial prints and solids, using the same techniques as for the flying fish hot pad.

Our pineapple and strawberry kitchen hangings shown on page 61 are also machine appliqued and could serve as hot pads, trivets, or wall hangings. These were faced and stuffed, but they would also be effective appliqued onto felt and hung as small banners.

Remember: any appliques done by hand (except for those using felt) *must* have a ¼-inch seam allowance added to *each* pattern piece to allow for turn-under.

Teapot in a Teapot Cosy

Materials: You'll need ½ yard *each* of light blue 100% cotton (or cotton/dacron blend), white cotton fabric for lining, and permanent-press muslin; ¼ yard white cotton or blend for teapot applique; ⅛ yard light brown cotton or blend for teapot handle applique; small green cotton scrap for leaf applique; small scrap of cotton or blend in blue floral print for flower applique and tab; 1 yard dacron batting 1-inch thick and 27 inches to 30 inches wide; 1 skein or ball each of pearl cotton in light brown, white, green, medium blue, and light blue; #7 darner needle; light blue sewing thread; scissors; sewing machine.

1) Enlarge teapot, handle, and flower designs; transfer to appropriate fabrics and cut them out, following hand applique directions on page 31.

2) Enlarge pattern for cosy and cut two pieces of light blue for cosy front and back, two of white for lining, 4 pieces of dacron batting, and two pieces of muslin for underlining.

3) Enlarge tab pattern and cut it out.

4) Applique teapot, handle, and flower to one layer of blue fabric, following hand applique instructions on page 31. Turn edges under and attach with matching pearl cotton thread, using a running stitch.

5) Make French knots in center of flower.

6) With muslin layer on the bottom, dacron batting in the middle, and blue fabric with applique on top, pin and baste all three layers together. Baste around curved edge only; do not baste bottom edge.

7) With pins perpendicular to quilting line, pin around area to be stitched. Using a quilting stitch (shown in illustration 58-A) in light blue pearl cotton, stitch along the quilting line.

8) Place white cotton lining on top of blue quilted piece (right sides together) and pin around curved edge. Machine stitch ½ inch from edge through all layers. Do not stitch bottom edge.

9) Trim ½ inch off curved edge of second piece of dacron batting. Place batting on top of white lining. When turned right side out, this second layer of batting will be between the lining and the muslin underlining. To keep batting in place permanently, whip stitch (see page 44) through all layers on their curved outside edge.

10) Turn right side out. Tuck in open edges at bottom ½-inch and slip stitch blue appliqued front to white lining.

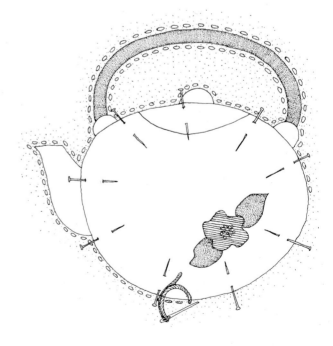

58-A quilting stitch

11) Enlarge and transfer cosy back design to other piece of blue fabric.

12) Following steps 6 through 10 above, quilt and assemble back of cosy.

13) Fold tab right sides together and machine stitch long edge ¼-inch from edge. Turn and press.

14) Fold tab in half; then baste to lining of tea cosy front so that 1 inch extends above top.

15) With linings together, turn in ½-inch seam allowance on curved edge and pin front and back together.

16) Slip stitch the two sides together, using light blue pearl cotton. Be sure to catch the tab securely.

Flying Fish Hot Pad

Materials: Use ½ yard gold corduroy or other preshrunk washable fabric; cotton or cotton/dacron blend scraps: green and white print fabric for fins, pink for cheek, blue fabric printed with a star or blue fabric and purchased star applique for eye, and 7 different color coordinated prints for gills; sewing thread; zigzag sewing machine; scissors; ½ yard cotton batting or large, old potholder for underlining; pins; water-base glue, plastic bag, or other bonding material to tack down applique (see "Hand and Machine Applique," page 30).

1) Enlarge design and transfer it to fabrics. Cut out 2 layers of yellow fabric for background shape.

2) Cut out shapes for cheek, eye, gills, and fins.

3) Pin, glue, or bond appliques in place on top of yellow fabric.

4) With brown thread and sewing machine, zigzag around all applique shapes; then zigzag a smile, as in the design.

5) Pin cotton batting to back of appliqued fabric and zig zag along outside edge of fish. Trim off excess batting.

6) Fold loop fabric in half lengthwise, right sides facing, and straight stitch ¼ inch in from edge. Turn and press. Next, pin loop in place on front of hot pad.

7) Pin fish front to back, right sides together.

8) With a straight stitch, carefully sew along outside edge of zigzag, leaving tail area open.

9) Trim seams to ¼ inch, turn to right side, and slip stitch tail closed.

Fruit Hang-Ups

Materials: Needed are ½ yard 100% pre-shrunk cotton or cotton/dacron blend fabric for front and back of fruit; cotton or blend scraps for leaf and fruit texture applique; ½ yard cotton batting; sewing thread; zigzag sewing machine; scissors; ½ yard cotton batting; pins; water-base glue, plastic bag, or bonding material to tack down applique (see "Hand and Machine Applique," page 30).

1) Enlarge design and transfer it to fabric.

2) Cut out two layers of cotton fabric for background shape; then cut out applique shapes. (Note: Applique pieces on pineapple skin are cut on the bias.)

3) Attach shapes by pinning or bonding them to background and then zigzag around them, following design below.

4) To complete, follow steps 6 through 9 on "Flying Fish," above, omitting step 7.

Numerals represent colors (see page 43)

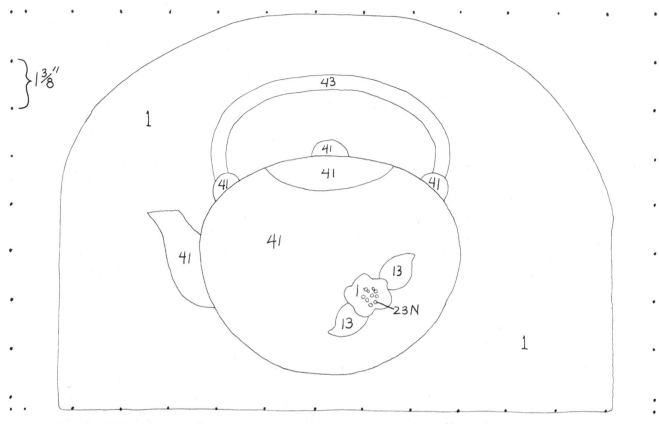

{ 1 3/8"

43

1

41

41

41

41

41

41

13

I

23N

13

1

Numerals represent colors (see page 43)
Letters represent stitches (see page 43)

Cool colors do a warm-up job on this appliqued
and quilted tea cosy. Heavy padding helps keep
tea and teapot warm for several hours. Directions
begin on page 58. Design: Ocean Beach Quilters:
Sonya Barrington and Suzanne Ish. Home Sweet
Home design on facing page, upper far right was
designed by Nancy Freeman.

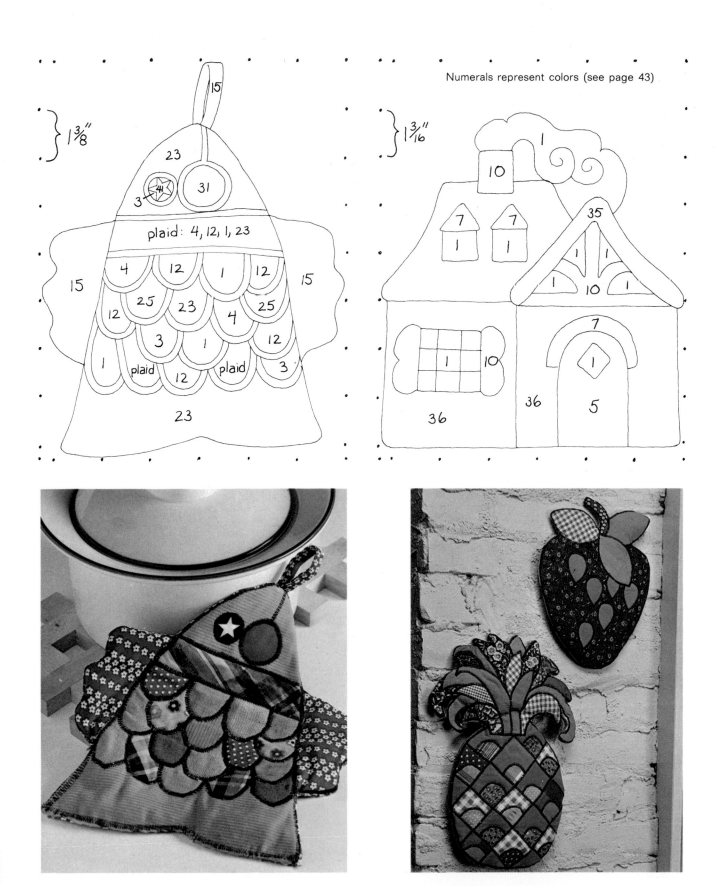

$1\frac{3}{8}''$

15

23

3 ← 41

31

plaid: 4, 12, 1, 23

15   4   12   1   12   15

12   25   23   4   25

12   3   1   12

1   plaid   12   plaid   3

23

$1\frac{3}{16}''$

1

10

7   7

1   1

35

1   1

1   10   1

7

1   10   1

36

36   5

Starry-eyed flying fish hot pad has its practical side; a heavy layer of cotton batting holds off the heat. Directions begin on page 59. Design: Nancy Freeman.

Purely decorative in intent, these cheery fruit hang-up decorations could also be hot pads in a pinch. Directions begin on page 59. Design: Nancy Freeman.

Bright and bold felt banners

(Color photos on page 64)

Each banner shown on page 64 is made of easy-to-handle felt and can be done up quickly either by hand or by machine.

"Welcome" not only expresses a greeting but also lets early-bird guests know they really *are* at the right house on the evening of a party. The center section saying "Welcome" could be backed with snaps or hook and pile tape so that it could be replaced with "Merry Christmas," "Happy Birthday," or a personal greeting.

"We Are What We Eat" can be a permanent decoration in the kitchen or breakfast room or saved for special occasions—perhaps the annual after-the-holidays diet?

For your favorite birthday boy/V.I.P., how about a felt mini-banner? A few felt scraps, beads, thread, and a safety pin for the back are all the materials required. For dimension, stuff between layers with cotton balls or dacron batting. Embroidery floss or several thicknesses of sewing thread can be used to present your message. The layers can be sewn together or glued or bonded. (See "Hand and Machine Applique," pages 30 to 33.) Other choices might be "Thanks," "Congratulations," "Be My Valentine," simple name tags, or place cards.

Welcome Banner

Materials: Get together 72-inch-wide felt: 2 yards red, ½ yard turquoise, ¾ yard purple, ½ yard magenta, ¾ yard orange; some dacron or cotton batting sewing thread to match felt colors; scissors; sewing machine; glue or bonding material (see "Hand and Machine Applique," page 30); or needle for hand sewing.

1) Enlarge design, transfer it to newspaper, then to felt. Draw two 7-inch squares and construct one large star in each square. Cut out stars and use as patterns for large three-dimensional stars.
2) Cut out felt shapes and arrange them on the red background; then pin them into place and sew down securely.
3) Stuff three-dimensional stars and letters with dacron or cotton batting before they are sewn shut and then attach to banner.
4) Cut out tabs and attach to top of banner if it will be hung from a painted dowel for display.

"We Are What We Eat"

Materials: Collect 60-inch or 72-inch-wide felt: ¾ yard of deep gold for background; ¼ yard of deep pink for pig; 6-inch felt squares (or small scraps) for flowers, ears, and nose: one each of lavender, deep pink, light pink, yellow, navy blue, light green, and white; four 6-inch squares of orange felt for lettering; pearl cotton: one each of orange, yellow, and green; sewing thread: one each of pink, orange, and navy blue; scissors; pins; sewing machine; scalloping or pinking shears (optional); 24-inch painted dowel for hanging.

1) Enlarge design and transfer to felt.
2) Cut out with pinking, scalloping, or regular scissors 2 large gold rectangles (18 by 24 inches) for background and three 3- by 6-inch rectangles for tabs.
3) Pin pig to center of banner. Sew around outside edge with sewing machine starting at back foot.
4) Sew inside curl of tail.
5) Sew on nose and ears with sewing machine.
6) Sew on eyes and nostrils by hand with matching thread.
7) Applique leaves and flowers to pig referring to stitch chart on page 43.
8) Attach letters by hand with sewing thread.
9) Iron banner on its wrong side with a warm iron.
10) Pin gold felt backing to front with right sides facing outward. Insert tabs between layers along top edge and pin them into place (see illustration 62-A).
11) Join felt pieces along all sides, sewing ½-inch from each edge.
12) Trim outside edges with pinking shears to even them, if necessary.
13) Thread with painted dowel and hang.

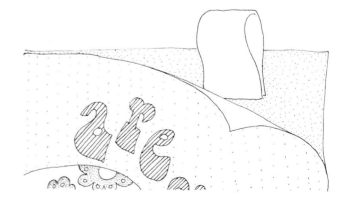

62-A attaching hanging tabs

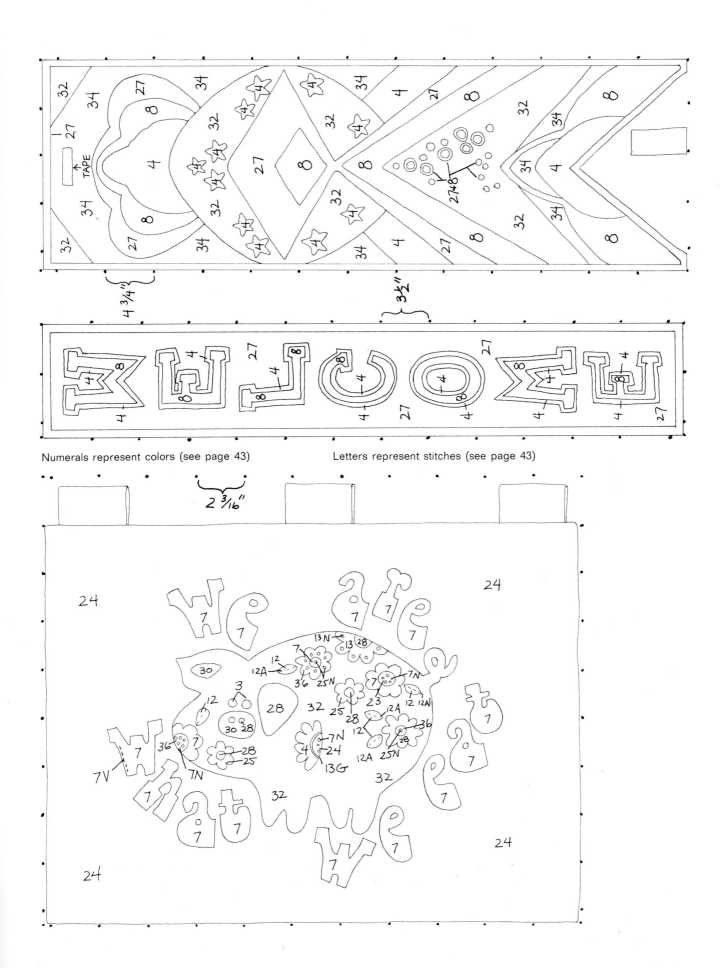

Numerals represent colors (see page 43)   Letters represent stitches (see page 43)

Special holidays can be commemorated with mini-banners in simple shapes made from felt. Here are two ideas to consider. *Design: Sally Paul.*

A star-studded welcome greets your guests when you hang out this brightly colored felt banner **(above)**. Hand and machine appliqued, it is simple to construct. Directions begin on page 62. *Design: Sally Paul.*

Humorous but gentle reminder to those who think with their stomachs, "We are What We Eat" banner suggests the consequences in felt applique and pearl cotton embroidery. Directions on page 62. *Design: Donna Yackey.*

Toys and dolls

(Color photos on page 67)

Sure to delight stuffed-toy fanciers and toy makers alike, the toys and dolls shown on the next two pages are very huggable. They're easily and quickly made.

The snap-on dolls shown on page 66 can be securely attached to your child's clothing or can be snapped onto the sleeping bag on page 70.

King of the Jungle

Materials: Assemble 1 yard of turquoise fabric; strands of Persian yarn in each color: 16 strands yellow, 6 brown, 4 dark green, 2 light green, 1 red; dacron batting for stuffing; crewel needle; turquoise sewing thread; sewing machine with zipper foot; scissors; pins.

1) Enlarge design and transfer it to fabric. Then reverse pattern to make a backing for lion.

2) Embroider front of lion. Use double thread for all areas except for eye, which is single thread.

3) Leaving ³/₄-inch seam allowances, cut out back and front of lion. Put right sides together, pin, and stitch on machine, using a zipper foot around mane so that embroidery isn't caught in seam. Leave bottom edge open. Trim seam to ¹/₂ inch.

4) Turn right side out and stuff lion. Turn in seam allowance on bottom edge and hand stitch seam.

5) Make yellow yarn tassels for tail, eyebrows, and whiskers (see quilt tying stitch, page 44).

6) Following diagram for back (68-A), take 5 yarn quilt ties to give dimension to the face.

Goldilocks Doll

Materials: Gather ¹/₄ yard pink, ¹/₄ yard white, and ¹/₂ yard gold felt, small scrap of blue felt for eyes; embroidered ribbon trim of your choice, 24 inches of each in ¹/₂-inch, 1¹/₂-inch, ³/₄-inch widths; 1 yard green ric rac; 24 inches of 1-inch-wide gathered eyelet trim; white, blue, and gold sewing thread; one skein of orange pearl cotton; 5 yards gold yarn for hair; 2 straw flowers; 1 foot of quarter-inch dowel; batting for stuffing; sewing machine; scissors; sewing needle; pins.

1) Enlarge design and transfer it to fabric. Add a ¹/₂-inch seam allowance to the outside edges only. Cut out all pieces. Using white thread, whip stitch (see page 44) bodice to neck only of head front and head back. Whip stitch lower edges of bodices to skirt front and skirt back.

2) Cut out all pieces. Using white thread, whip stitch (see page 44) bodice to neck only of head front and head back. Whip stitch lower edges of bodices to skirt front and skirt back.

3) By machine, sew ribbons and eyelet to skirt front and skirt back, matching ribbons at side seams.

4) Apply ric rac with a running stitch in orange pearl cotton along neck of bodice and over eyelet lace.

5) Whip stitch eyes to face with blue sewing thread.

6) Backstitch an orange pearl cotton smile on face.

7) Press; then carefully pin doll with its right sides together, matching front and back appliques. Leaving a ¹/₂-inch seam allowance, stitch the doll together, using a sewing machine. Leave bottom edge of doll open.

8) Trim seams, clip curves; then turn doll right side out.

9) Stuff head and arms, using a dowel to push the batting into place. Fill rest of doll.

10) Whip stitch bottom edge closed. Sew on yarn hair with sewing thread. Tack a few tendrils to shoulders and tie them in back with grosgrain ribbon.

11) Tack right hand to skirt; then slip straw flowers under hand and tack them down.

Russian Princess Doll

Materials: Collect ¹/₄ yard dark turquoise, ¹/₈ yard mauve, ¹/₈ yard purple, ¹/₈ yard light turquoise, ¹/₈ yard dark green washable velveteen; seam binding: 1 package each of light orange, mauve, magenta; ⁵/₈-inch-wide velvet ribbon: ¹/₄ yard rust; small scrap of chamois or felt for face; pearl cotton: one skein each of magenta, light orange, rust; sewing thread: dark turquoise, green, light turquoise, mauve, purple; batting for stuffing; sewing machine; scissors; needle; pins; cardboard for base.

1) Enlarge design and transfer it to fabric, adding a ¹/₄-inch seam allowance to each pattern piece, except for chamois. Cut out velvet pieces and chamois.

2) Turning edges under ¹/₄ inch, first applique green and then light turquoise vertical panels to center front bodice of doll. Embroider design on center front panel, following stitch and color guides.

3) Attach chamois face to head with a blanket stitch. Embroider face.

4) Applique seam binding horizontally below face, turning under raw edges only. (Overlap face and center front panel with top and bottom binding.)

5) Right sides facing, pin mauve hands and light turquoise cuffs together and sew. Open right side out. Next, pin gloves and cuffs to deep blue bodice, front and back.

6) Turn edges under ¹/₄ inch and slip stitch (page 54) vertical purple and green velvet strips to girdle front. With a running stitch in pearl cotton, attach seam

binding and velvet ribbon vertically to the girdle on the front and back of the doll.

7) Turning under seam allowance, slip stitch girdle to bodice and head front and back.

8) Turn edges under and slip stitch girdle to purple lower skirt, the lower skirt to blue scallops, and scallops to green bottom panel on front of doll. Repeat for doll's back.

9) Embroider lower edge of scallops front and back.

10) Pin front to back with right sides together, matching panels at side seams. Stitch, leaving bottom edge open. Trim seams; clip curves.

11) Turn doll right side out and stuff.

12) Cut a piece of cardboard ¼ inch smaller than the oval green fabric base. Gather edge of fabric base around cardboard and press with a warm iron.

13) Slip stitch fabric-covered base to bottom of doll.

Snap-On Toys

Materials: Collect less than ¼ yard each of permanent-press fabric remnants or scraps for clothes, dolls, and accessories; white doublefold bias tape; yarn; embroidery floss; buttons and felt scraps; sewing thread; needle; scissors; sewing machine; flannel or batting. Bicycle frame: 4 pipe cleaners; 18 inches of blue velvet cording.

To make basic doll:

1) Enlarge pattern and transfer it to fabric. Cut out shapes. With right sides facing, sew seams on body and head (for bike boy, leave body unsewn from waist down). Clip seams, turn, and stuff both pieces.

2) Embroider face, tack yarn to head, and slip stitch head to body.

3) Stitch side seams of dress for girl or shirt for boy, leaving an opening at the neck large enough to fit over doll's head; turn and put on body. Slip stitch back seam opening to neck.

4) Cut 1¼-inch lengths of bias tape to fit around each neck. Fold in half lengthwise; then slip stitch edges and tack around to front of neck.

5) With right sides facing, stitch sleeve side seams. Clip, turn, and stuff. Slip stitch to body front and back.

6) Slip stitch hands and feet to body of girl doll and hands only for bike boy. Sew a snap on the doll's back.

7) Decorate dress with French knot "buttons." Arrange hair on girl and make a felt book.

To make bicycle:

1) Cut four circles of white fabric for wheels, stitch, turn, and stuff. Slip stitch edges closed. Make spokes with embroidery floss. Cut two shapes for print fabric bike body. Stitch, turn, and stuff. Slip stitch opening.

2) Remove cording from inside the velvet tubing and cut tubing in these lengths: 2½ inches, handlebars; ½ inch, handlebar shaft; 1½ inches, seat bar; 3 inches, front wheel shaft; 4½ inches, pedal and chain shaft; 1½ inches, back wheel shaft. Stuff with pipe cleaners. Shape and attach to wheels and print fabric bike body.

3) Stitch legs of doll to bike frame, hands to handlebars. Then applique slacks over boy's legs on each side and slip stitch shirt over raw waistband of pants. Attach feet. Sew buttons to center of bike wheels.

Snap-on doll becomes a child's permanent companion when attached to her pocket or to the quilt shown on page 70. Directions above. Design: Barbara Benson.

Bike boy snap-on doll enjoys nothing more than a ride around the park on his pipe-cleaner bike (see page 70). Directions begin above. Design: Barbara Benson.

Crewel-countenanced lion is as comfortable napping on your couch as in the African bush. Directions begin on page 65. Design: Sue and Robert Hostick.

Goldilocks, dressed up in her beribboned, embroidered felt gown, is thinking of anything but the three bears. Directions on page 65. Design: Donna Yackey.

Richly attired Russian princess could have stepped from the pages of a child's fairy tale. Directions on page 65. Based upon a design by Katherine Fukami Glascock.

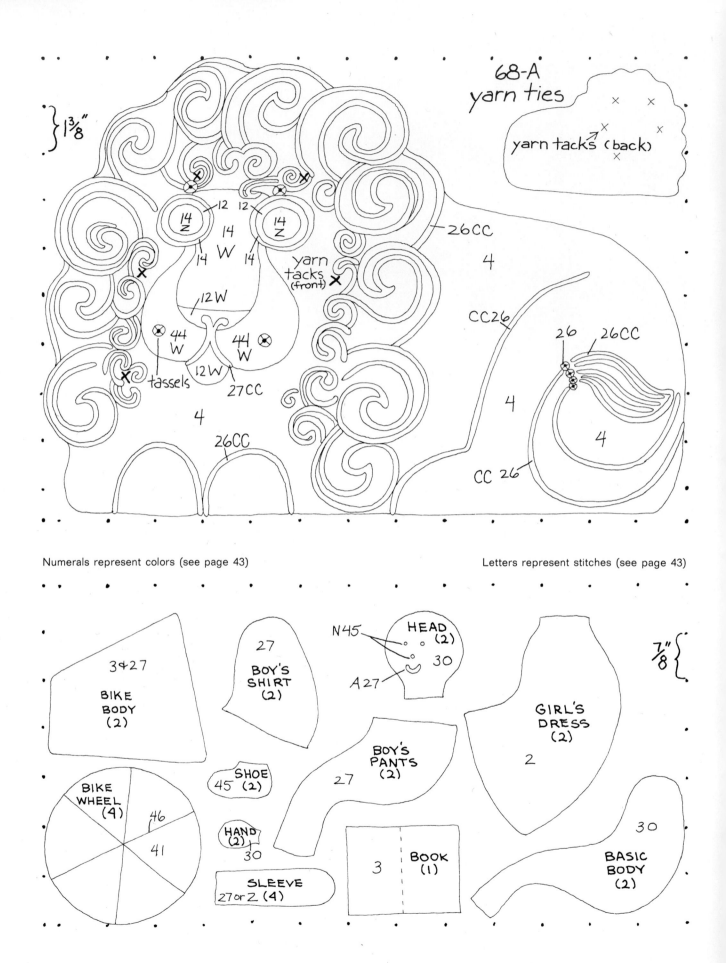

68-A
yarn ties

yarn tacks (back)

1 3/8"

14 Z   12   12   14 Z
14   14 W   14
26CC
4
12W
yarn tacks (front)
CC26
26 26CC
44 W   44 W
12W
tassels   27CC
4
4
4
4
26CC

Numerals represent colors (see page 43)   Letters represent stitches (see page 43)

34 27
BIKE BODY (2)

27
BOY'S SHIRT (2)

N45   HEAD (2)
30
A 27

7/8"

GIRL'S DRESS (2)
2

BIKE WHEEL (4)
46
41

SHOE 45 (2)

HAND (2)
30

BOY'S PANTS (2)
27

BOOK (1)
3

30
BASIC BODY (2)

SLEEVE
27 or 2 (4)

68   PROJECTS: TOYS AND DOLLS

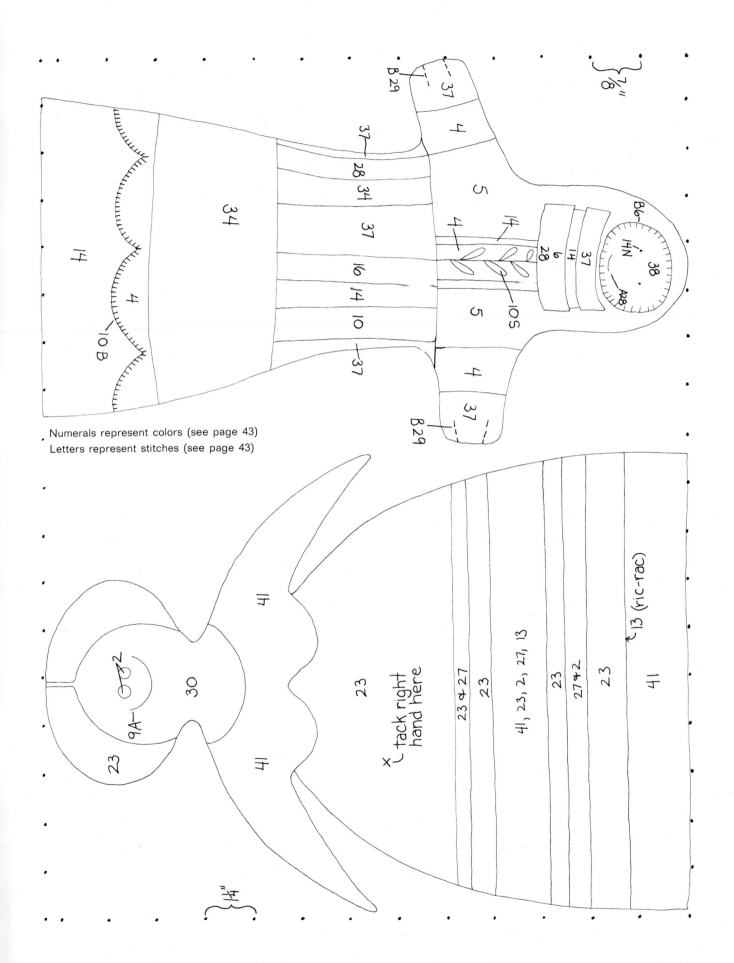

Numerals represent colors (see page 43)
Letters represent stitches (see page 43)

Fantasy landscape quilt *becomes a sleeping bag quick as a wink; just climb in and zip, tape, or snap shut. An industrial zipper, hook and pile tape, or heavy-duty snaps do the trick when transforming the quilt into a slumber-party or nap bag. Snap-on dolls (see page 66) enliven the landscape. Trucks and cars are easily made in the same manner as the hot pads on page 61. Directions on facing page. Design: Barbara Benson. Concept: Sylvia Matthews.*

Scenic sleeping bag

Purple gingham mountain majesties topped with dollops of white cotton snow dominate the cheery road map quilt shown on page 70. When folded in half, the hook-and-pile tape sewn around three edges closes the quilt into a sleeping bag for slumber parties or overnight guests.

Although photographed on a lawn, the sleeping bag isn't really meant for outdoor use since the fabric was not weatherproofed.

The quilt top is assembled from the top downward to give a feeling of dimension. Completely assembled before being attached to a stuffed backing, it could be put over an old sleeping bag (with a good zipper), a comforter, or a comforter kit (sold through mail-order back-packing and camping catalogues).

The two dolls and the truck have snaps sewn to their back sides and to the quilt. You could also sew snaps to a favorite pair of pajamas for the dolls to ride on.

For directions on making the dolls, see page 66. To make the truck or a car (as shown on page 72), simply cut out two thicknesses of printed fabric, sew them together, turn, and stuff with a layer of flannel. Make the eight wheels the same way. Decorate with buttons and scraps of fabric.

Materials: Gather together comforter or sleeping bag to be covered; permanent-press cotton/blend fabric for applique: 2 yards of dark green for grass, 1-1/3 yards medium green for grass and hills, 1/2 yard of medium dark

An overnight out of doors? Just plan to first put down a tarp or plastic drop cloth to protect your embroidery and applique efforts from the dampness of the grass.

Position snap-on dolls (see page 66) wherever you wish, as well as any trucks or cars that happen to drive by. Pattern for a car may be found on the following page.

green for hills, ½ yard of light green for bushes and trees; 3 light green prints, ¼ yard each for trees and bushes; 2 dark green prints, ¼ yard each for night bushes and trees; ⅛ yard of purple for rainbow, ¼ yard of yellow for sun, moon, and rainbow, ⅛-yard pink for rainbow, 1⅓ yard of light blue for lake, sky, and river, ½ yard dark blue for sky, 1¼ yards of gray for road and side of lake, ¾ yard of purple gingham for mountains, ⅓ yard of brown for tree trunks and bridge, ½ yard of white for cloud, snow, and road strips; sewing thread to match all of the colors listed above; needle, scissors; snaps for dolls; 3¼ yards of hook-and-pile tape to make comforter into a sleeping bag (omit if you plan to use a sleeping bag with a zipper); sewing machine; metallic thread for stars; dacron batting to stuff trees and bushes. (See snap-on dolls, page 66, for materials and instructions for dolls.)

1) Enlarge design at far right and transfer it to butcher paper or newspaper, adding ¼-inch seam allowances to edges which will be turned under.

2) Preshrink fabric and comforter before tracing and cutting out patterns.

3) Cut out shapes, following paper patterns. Then run a row of machine stitching ¼ inch in from edges to be turned. Press edge under ¼ inch with a warm iron, clipping curves where necessary.

4) For bridge, cut a 12- by 7-inch rectangle of brown cloth. Pin tuck eight ⅛-inch overlaps set 1 inch apart along the 12-inch length of the rectangle and then sew down the overlaps(see 72-A).

5) Seam light and dark sky pieces together on the sewing machine.

6) Applique white tops of mountains to purple gingham by hand (with a running stitch or back stitch).

7) Pin cloud, moon, and sun to sky; stitch.

8) Stitch rainbow pieces together by machine. Pin in place and sew down. Applique and embroider face on sun; embroider stars; applique eye on moon.

9) Attach mountains and small green hill at upper left to sky and to one another. Stitch into place.

10) Applique pine trees and trunks to light green hill; applique white dashes to top portion of gray road piece. Pin all green hills and road together above the river and bridge. Whip stitch pieces together.

11) Pin upper edge of hills to mountains and sky. Stitch.

12) Pin river in place along lower edge of hills. Sew down.

13) It may be necessary to join two widths of light green fabric to make a piece of fabric large enough for the lower left-hand area of the quilt. Do so, and then join it to the lower edge of the river.

14) Applique white dashes to lower road.

15) Pin road to light green grass and to dark green grass. Sew to lower edge of river.

16) Pin bridge in place. Stitch it down.

17) Pin gray border to pond. Stitch. Pin entire pond in place. Stitch it down.

18) Pin three green bushes together; stuff them slightly and stitch them to grass above lake. Repeat with other two bushes.

19) Pin treetop pieces together for each of the four remaining trees. Stuff them slightly and applique them to grass. Pin tree trunks in place, stuff, and stitch them to grass and treetops.

20) Now that design is completely assembled, turn under the raw edges around all outside edges and pin it to comforter. Machine stitch cover to comforter.

21) Starting at center top of the wrong side of the quilt, pin a length of tape with fiber "hooks" across top, down one side, and back to the center of the *bottom* of the quilt. Pin pile on fuzzy length of tape, starting at center top of wrong side of quilt and going down and along untaped edge to the center of the bottom edge of the quilt. Machine stitch along both edges of tape.

22) To make dolls, see page 66.

72-A fabric tucks for bridge

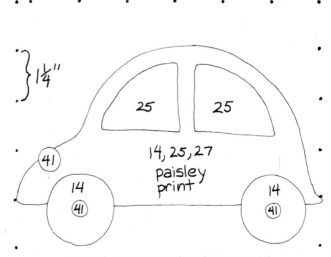

Numerals represent colors (see page 43)

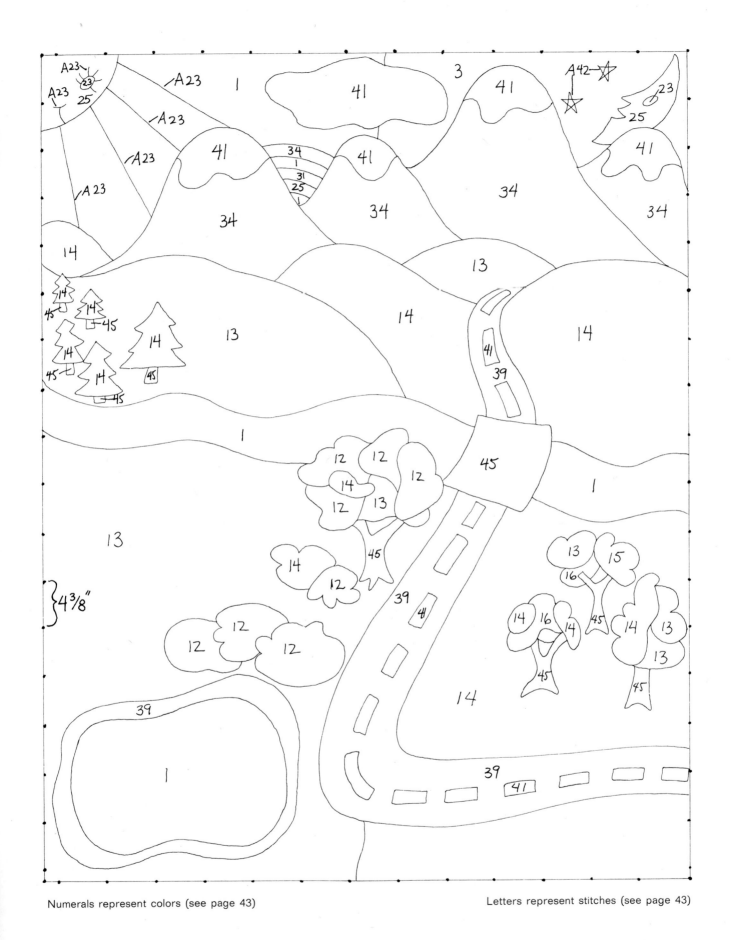

Numerals represent colors (see page 43)

Letters represent stitches (see page 43)

Experiments in stitchery

The stitchery ideas shown on these pages are here to inspire you. Trying new directions and developing your own ideas can bring satisfaction even to the experienced stitcher. It can also be a fun way to introduce skeptical novices to an exciting craft that doesn't have to be limited to embroidered hankies and tedious "Home Sweet Home" samplers.

As you begin to do your own designing, be sure to include your signature (or initials) and the completion date on a corner of the piece; hand-made crafts have a way of lasting for several generations!

1) Use stitchery to personalize professional uniforms by adding an embroidered cartoon or flower. Doctors, dentists, and nurses immediately become less formidable with a smiling sun and rainbow decorating their pockets or lapels.

2) Make rubbings from tombstones, manhole covers, and stone plaques; they're perfect subjects for stitchery. Transfer the design to cloth and simply outline the shapes in stitchery.

3) Make a sketch of your home or favorite building from life or a photograph. Transfer the design to cloth and stitch. Many civic groups do this with favorite landmarks and sell printed canvases to the community as a fund raiser. Also see facing page.

4) Use heavy yarns (such as rug yarn) to fill in areas on a large piece—say a piano bench cover. Couched with lightweight yarn, these greatly resemble Mexican Huichol yarn and beeswax "paintings."

5) Let lettering add to the impact of a stitchery. Look for good examples in newspaper and magazine advertising or invest in type design books or books specializing in needlepoint and cross stitch alphabets. Enlarge them, if necessary, and transfer them to fabric. Outline them with split stitch or back stitch. Fill in with satin stitch, seeding, or other fill-in stitches (See the chart on page 12). Backstitch and running stitch (when tacked down occasionally) both adapt well to alphabets.

6) Translate a marriage or birth announcement into a stitchery hanging. Copy the actual announcement or make up your own design, perhaps using one of the designs on pages 46 to 52 for decoration. Use backstitch or cross stitch to "write" the information.

7) Have a favorite old photograph enlarged, transfer the basic outlines to fabric, embroider the design, and then frame or make a pillow from the stitchery.

Quilted planter cover is a real eye-stopper. Dyed, stuffed, and stitched, this surreal skyscape on a cup proudly bears two golden ceramic stars. Design: Sue Bender.

"It's a super suit" lapel decoration combines baby beads, commercial applique, twine, and Superman. Design: Margaret A. Sahlstrand.

8) Trim ski parkas with embroidery or applique for a unique decoration and positive identification on the slopes.

9) Use a Mexican wedding shirt as the base for a sampler. Each tuck on the front panel can be embroidered with a different stitch. For a festive look, use lots of bright colors.

10) Make plant "cosys" to cover clay pots using washable fabric for the cover and applique. Patchwork applique or hand and machine embroidery are also effective decorations. See photo on facing page.

11) Experiment with colors and print combinations from your scrap box when planning applique projects. See the cheerful gingham shirt below.

12) Try new directions and combine stitchery with other media such as blue-printing, indelible markers, fabric paints, or commercial fabric dye (see the planter cosy on facing page). All add color quickly and a new dimension.

13) Buy a kit in a hobby or art supply store for transferring printed material (from magazines, newspapers, posters, wrapping paper, or calendars) to fabric. The kits contain specially treated paper, a solution for transferring the ink on the page to your fabric, and all the necessary tools.

14) Investigate the new machine that has been developed to transfer color images to fabric (sometimes called wash and wear color prints). Almost any source can be used for the transfer; slides, photographs, drawings, book jackets, posters, even three-dimensional objects. The transfer is done instantly (it is a reverse image) and can be put on fabric, canvas, leather, and wood. The cost is about $5.00 for a 8½- by 11-inch design. Look for this service in the telephone book yellow pages under "copying and duplicating services."

15) Don't overlook ready-made appliques. When they are combined with stitchery, beads, and buttons, the result can be an amusing collage for a T-shirt or denim jacket. (See the photo on facing page.)

16) Try writing your name and then make a Rorschach ink blot-like mirror image of it. Combine the two with embroidered flowers for a unique and personal design for a purse, shopping bag, or bike bag.

17) Make a favorite object into a table sculpture. How about a stuffed tennis shoe? A favorite old hat bean bag? Or a stuffed satin replica of your first car?

Stuffed and stitched, "Lucille" **(top)** is the neighborhood's most friendly pooch. Design: Kay M. Aronson. "Friendly Farm" **(bottom)**, a print on print hand-applique, is a favorite local landmark of the artist's. Design: Janny Burghardt.

Printed fabric appliques spruce up purchased shirt **(top).** Design: Ocean Beach Quilters: Sonya Barrington and Suzanne Ish. "Mirror Mirror on the Wall" **(bottom)** has a crewel-covered mirror frame. Design: Nancy Wriggle.

Buon gusto kitchen sampler

(Color photo on page 78)

"Buon Gusto" means "Eat Heartily." Every cook who shares this sentiment about her efforts in the kitchen will want to make this sampler as pictured on page 78. Embroidered birds and bees grace this wall decoration, along with spices, herbs, fruits, and vegetables—everything a good cook likes to keep on hand in her well stocked pantry. There are even two kinds of grapes to please the wine connoisseur.

The list of materials calls for three kinds of embroidery thread and 21 colors. Feel free to vary or simplify this list to suit your personal tastes or your kitchen decor.

Directions are given for the frame shown in the photograph. It is actually two frames: the completed sampler is stretched around and tacked to a redwood frame. A second redwood frame is then constructed and slipped over the sampler to complete the project. You may wish to make only the inner frame or to stretch your completed sampler around stretcher bars as was done for the sampler shown on the cover. (See "Finishing," pages 34 to 35, for instructions and information on stretcher bars.)

Materials: You'll need ⅜ yard of off-white polyester/cotton fabric; #5 pearl cotton, one skein each of: gold, olive green, peach; #8 pearl cotton, one skein each: rust, olive green, medium brown, light gold, dark brown, grey, and maroon; one skein each of embroidery floss in dark grey, peach, magenta, light apple green, red, ecru, purple, medium green, green-gold, dark blue-green, grey-green; embroidery needles and hoop; curved upholstery needle; heavy duty sewing thread.

For the frame, here's what you'll need: #3 upholstery tacks (¼ inch long); 4d finishing nails (1½ inches long); 80 inches of redwood 1 by 1 (actually measures ¾ by ¾ inches); white glue; saw-tooth picture hanger and ½-inch brads; sandpaper; oil, wax, or varnish.

1) Enlarge design (given on page 78) and transfer it to white fabric.

2) Embroider sampler, following stitch and color guide.

3) Soak finished piece in lukewarm, sudsy water; rinse well.

4) Roll it in a towel to remove excess water. Unroll it and stretch it slightly with your hands in both directions to pull out wrinkles. Dry it flat on a towel.

5) When dry, steam iron it face down on a dry towel.

6) To make inner frame, cut four ¾-inch by ¾-inch redwood strips (called 1 by 1's) to form a rectangle 6 inches by 13 inches (outside dimensions). Glue and nail them together with finishing nails.

7) With sampler face down on a flat surface, center frame over back side of sampler. Stretch fabric around frame and tack it at back of frame with ¼-inch upholstery tacks. Begin by tacking fabric to the top and bottom centers of the frame; then fold side edges in as if wrapping a package and tack the sides at the centers. Stretch evenly and tack toward corners, working away from the centers so you finish at all four corners at once. Don't complete one corner at a time. Alternate from corner to corner as you work so that the sampler will not be warped out of shape. Trim fabric, leaving a ½-inch excess.

8) Make an outer frame by cutting four ¾-inch by ¾-inch redwood strips to fit flush around stretched embroidery. Remove the outer frame and assemble it separately. Sand and finish it with oil, wax, or varnish. When it is dry, slip the outer frame around the stretched sampler and tack through both frames with finishing nails.

9) From leftover fabric, cut a 7- by 14-inch backing; iron under ½ inch on all sides. Using a curved needle and heavy duty thread, sew it to fabric stretched around back side, inside the outer frame.

10) With brads, tack a sawtooth picture hanger to the inner frame.

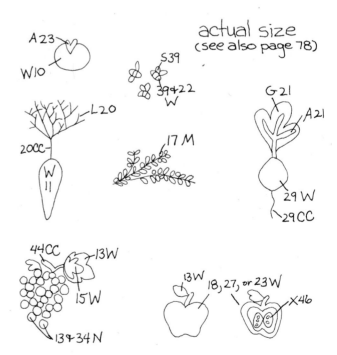

Numerals represent colors (see page 43)
Letters represent stitches (see page 43)

Art deco dress

(Color photo on page 79)

The delightful art deco design shown in the photo on page 79 is reminiscent of 1930s movie theaters, marcelled hair, and funky jewelry. The icy pastels of the embroidered design melt into the mauve of this long polyester dress. Black, silver, or white would also be appropriate colors for the dress and embroidery.

Materials: Collect 3 skeins each of embroidery floss in pale yellow, blue green, salmon pink, medium purple, and light leaf green; one skein pale mauve; embroidery needle; embroidery hoop; scissors; ready-made or home made dress.

1) Enlarge design and transfer it to dress or fabric. Transfer is more simple if the dress is not yet constructed,

as in a home-made dress; otherwise, try to remove the side seams to allow the cloth to be laid out flat for transfer. The design can be repeated on the back of the dress for a 360-degree effect; if you decide to do so, avoid interrupting the design with a long zipper. (The dress shown has an invisible zipper in the left shoulder seam.)

2) Embroider dress or fabric, following stitch and color guides found on the pattern. Begin embroidery in outlines first, using a satin stitch; then fill in larger areas with indicated decorative stitches. Embroider all but two inches on either side of side seams. Sew up side seams, matching design if a 360-degree plan is used. Complete embroidery over seams before you go on to finish the rest of the dress.

Numerals represent colors (see page 43)
Letters represent stitches (see page 43)

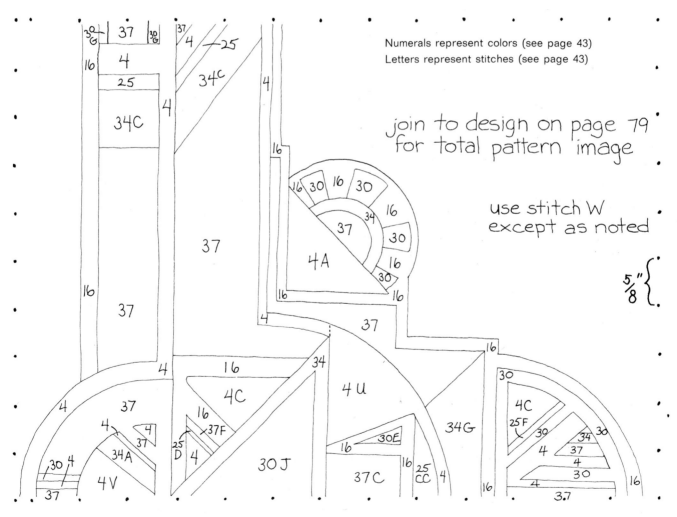

join to design on page 79 for total pattern image

use stitch W except as noted

"Buon Gusto" is the confident declaration of the accomplished gourmet cook. Here on this herb, vegetable, and fruit-decorated wall plaque, it hints of good things to come from the kitchen. Design: Linda Ridella.

Numerals represent colors (see page 43)
Letters represent stitches (see page 43)

actual size

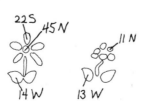

16

30G

34 4

5/8" {

16 4

16

25

16

37 4

34 4

34

16

join
design
here →

30
G

37

30
G

4

37

4

4 4

25

16

4

25

34C

34C

37

16

Numerals represent colors (see page 43)
Letters represent stitches (see page 43)

Pastel color combination *enhances the clean, geometric appeal of this 1930s-inspired decorative embroidery. Bright colors or a monochromatic scheme could replace these colors, if desired. Design: Alyson Smith Gonsalves.*

Index

Photographers

Kay M. Aronson: 75 (upper left). **David Beamer:** 37 (upper left, lower right), 38 (upper left). **Ann Ammons Bryant:** 33 (upper left), 36 (lower right), 38 (lower left). **Janny Burghardt:** 40 (lower right), 75 (lower left). **George Chang:** 40 (lower left). **Glenn Christiansen:** 49 (all), 52 (all), 53 (all), 56, 57, 60, 61 (all), 64 (all), 66 (all), 67 (all), 70, 71 (all), 74 (left), 75 (upper left), 78, 79. **Dennis DeSilva—Studio 7:** 38 (lower right). **Allan Feller:** 41 (lower left). **Jill Friedrick:** 36 (upper right), 38 (upper right). **Nancy Gano:** 40 (upper left). **Alyson Smith Gonsalves:** 15 (all). **Doris Hoover:** 39 (lower right). **Harold House:** 36 (lower left). **John Huddleson:** 39 (upper left). **Prudy Kohler:** 36 (upper left). **Ells Marugg:** 33 (lower left, upper right). **Kirby Moulton:** 37 (lower left), 40 (upper right). **Barbara Neill:** 37 (upper right). **Norman A. Plate:** 5 (upper left, center, and right). **James M. Sahlstrand:** 41 (upper right), 74 (right). **Lee Sammis:** 39 (lower left). **Roz Shirley:** 39 (upper right). **Kay Shuper:** 41 (lower right). **John Svoboda:** 33 (lower right), 41 (upper left). **Darrow M. Watt:** 4 (all), 5 (bottom), 6, 7, 8, 10, 11, 14, 27, 29, 34, 35, 42. **Larry Wriggle:** 75 (lower right).